Books should be returned or renewed by the last date
above. Renew by phone **08458 247 200** or online
www.kent.gov.uk/libs

Libraries & Archives

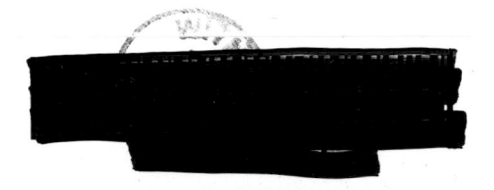

THE BESIEGED

THE
BESIEGED
A STORY OF SURVIVAL

CAROLINE WALTON

Biteback Publishing

First published in Great Britain in 2011 by
Biteback Publishing Ltd
Westminster Tower
3 Albert Embankment
London
SE1 7SP

isbn 978-1-84954-147-3
10 9 8 7 6 5 4 3 2 1

A CIP catalogue record for this book is available from the
British Library.

Set in Caslon and Univers by Namkwan Cho
Cover design by Namkwan Cho

Printed and bound in Great Britain
by CPI Group (UK) Ltd, Croydon, CR0 4YY

To the blokadniki

In Pursuit of Someone Drifting Down the Icy Neva

It was 1942.
I was reeling
From hunger,
From longing,
From grief.
But spring came in,
    – Unmoved
By my troubles.
Broken into shards,
Like lump sugar,
Ice from the Road of Life,
Floated down the Neva.
And from Liteiny Bridge
I saw
Somewhere in the middle of the
    Neva,
On the gently pitching ice,
The distinct shape
Of a cross.
The ice drifted
Beyond the piers
It slowed before the bridge.
Cruciform,
With arms spread out,
A figure lay welded into the ice.
No not a soldier killed at
    Dubrovka
On the accursed Nevsky field,
But a little boy,
Childishly awkward,
In a belted kurguz jacket.
How he died on Ladoga
I don't know.
Killed by a bullet or frozen in a
    blizzard.

…Over the seas,
His crystal bed floats,
Melting a little at the edges.
He drifts beneath the light of
    Constellations,
As though in a cradle,
On a grey wave.
…I have seen the world.
Circled half the earth,
Time has stripped my soul bare.
Children laughed
In London.
School kids danced
In Antofagasta.
But he
Drifted on into unknown
    regions,
Like a soft moan
Through a mother's sleep.
Lands were shaken by
    earthquakes.
Volcanoes choked.
Bombs wailed.
And souls were numbed.
But he drifted on in his cradle
    of glass.
My soul shall have no rest.
Forever,
Everywhere,
Asleep and awake,
As long as I live,
I shall drift with him through
    the world,
I shall drift through human
    memory.

Mikhail Dudin, 1966

CONTENTS

ACKNOWLEDGEMENTS

I am deeply grateful to Helena Abram of the Galatea Trust for financing my research in St Petersburg. I am indebted to all those siege survivors named in this book who so generously shared their time, memories and food with me. I would also like to thank Alexandra Vlasova and Tatiana Valerich for revealing Petersburg to me. Natalia Tarasova kindly granted permission to include her aunt Anna Alexeeva's poems. Vladimir Schnittke of the Petersburg Memorial Society introduced me to Tamara Petkevich. The staff of the Anichkov Palace, above all Larissa Viktorievna and Larissa Rudolfevna, were extremely helpful in making introductions. I would also like to thank my friend Anna Annenkova for opening doors on many levels, Max Arthur for encouraging me to write the book in its current form, Dr Mike Jones for his comments on an early draft, Jill Robinson for her unfailing support with the writing. Special thanks go to my agent Peter Buckman. Finally, it has been a joy to work with my editor at Biteback Sam Carter. On a personal note, my thanks go to John Irwin and Andrei Walton.

AUTHOR'S NOTE

The city of St Petersburg was founded in 1703 by Tsar Peter the Great. During the First World War it was given the Russified name of Petrograd. Following the revolution of 1917 the city was renamed Leningrad. After a referendum in 1991 it reverted to St Petersburg.

Russians have a first name, a patronymic, and a family name. Thus: Yelena Vyacheslavovna (the daughter of Vyacheslav) Vlasova. People are most commonly addressed by their first names and patronymics. Diminutives of the first name are also very commonly used, e.g. Lena, Lenochka for Yelena.

Names and some details of younger characters and people personally connected to me have been changed.

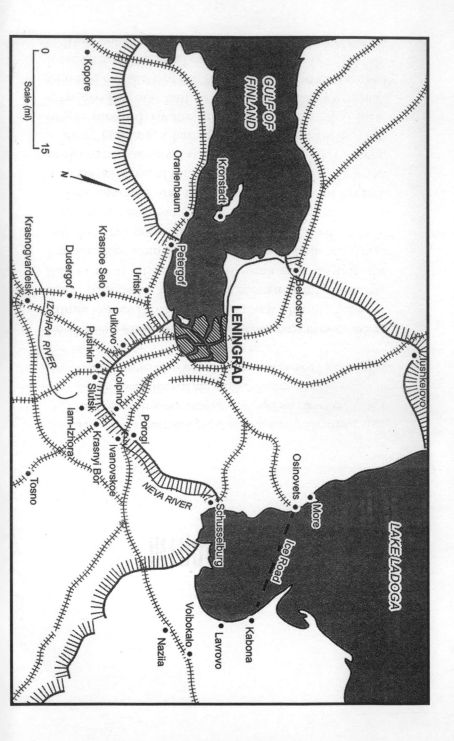

INTRODUCTION

*It is a bitter truth that the spiritual secret of the siege
will disappear along with us. Although we ourselves
have not yet fathomed this secret to its depths.*
Oleg Shestinskii – poet and siege survivor

L ondon, Coventry, Dresden, Hiroshima; in more recent
times Port au Prince, New York, New Orleans, Sarajevo,
Kobe, Baghdad… But never in human history has a city
lost so many of its people as Leningrad. During the
872-day siege from 8 September 1941 to 27 January 1944
half the city's population of three million died, most of
them from starvation.

One hundred and twenty five grammes of bread a
day, temperatures of minus 30 degrees, no running water
or electricity, cannibals stalking the streets, NKVD spies
in every building, a barrage of bombs and shells… yet
people survived. By the time the siege was lifted there
remained just over half a million *blokadniki* – survivors
who had neither died nor been evacuated to unoccupied
Russia across the Road of Life.

This book asks – how? What enables people to

survive extreme circumstances – physically, mentally, emotionally and spiritually? Unfortunately the question is as relevant today as it was in the nineteen forties.

Most of the *blokadniki* who spoke to me so freely about their experiences are now dead. It is my hope and wish that the spiritual secret of the siege might not disappear with them.

This book is dedicated to their memory.

1

Oh Pushkin's beloved city
How far off those years are now!
You fell, tortured, into an abyss…
Vladimir Nabokov – *Petersburg*

The human struggle against despair is nothing new.

These words circle my head like flies. I look down again at the book on my lap, a collection of letters and poems written during the siege of Leningrad.

The struggle against despair is an inherent feature of our existence.

My train is announced. I shove the book into my bag and shuffle through a neon-lit limbo towards the escalator. The Eurostar glides out from a ghostly morning platform. London Waterloo, the British Interplanetary Society, faded graffiti on black brick: *Punk Rules*, concrete tenements, the four sentinels of Battersea power station, a lone spotter on Clapham Junction. Commuters keep silent vigil on suburban stations. Mist hangs low over fields, abruptly pierced by wire fencing and watch towers. We are swallowed by the tunnel. A passenger rises from his seat across the aisle and takes a picture of the darkness through the window.

The train's familiar motion lulls me into a doze. I awaken somewhere on the outskirts of Lille. It is 1999 and I am travelling back to St Petersburg. Go, a friend urged, go and write about the siege.

The siege of Leningrad has haunted me since my first visit to the city as a student in 1979. On a chilly April morning, melting snow running in rivulets over tarmac, I stood by the Monument to Victory with bowed head, listening to the Intourist guide describe the mass starvation of a city so like my own.

Later I became involved with a man who bore the siege's legacy. The son of a survivor, Ivan Nikolaevich was a native of Samara, a provincial city on the Volga. I first met him there in 1992 while researching a book on post-Soviet Russia. He invited me to see *Eugene Onegin*, then walked me home along the misty river.

I returned to London. A phone call came. Ivan wanted to send me an invitation. Didn't I miss the Volga? At the sound of his voice my London life ebbed like grey tidewater. I abandoned my home and work and bought a ticket to Samara, changing in Moscow and heading eastwards through Ryazan and over the wide Volga. As a blizzard raged across the steppe I felt the vertiginous joy of hurtling through boundless space. Today that excitement has vanished without trace, as completely as a disgraced comrade from a Stalin-era photograph. In the end I stayed with Ivan for no more than a few months.

Brussels Midi. Another half-world, a subterranean antechamber insulated by glass from the life of the city. The overhead screen flickers a summons. I board a pristine train that glides through immaculate landscapes, over the Rhine bridge and into Köln Hauptbahnhof. I alight into a swarm of rucksacks and suitcases bound for Munich or Paris. The piles of zipped plastic carrier bags on platform eight tell me where the Moscow train comes in.

'Will I have it to myself?' I ask the Russian attendant who brings freshly-laundered sheets to my compartment. He sifts through a sheaf of papers. 'For tonight.' He twirls his pen. 'I can put someone in with you though. So you won't be lonely.'

Two nights and a day will take me to the capital; from there I will catch the overnight *Arrow* express north. Berlin Zoo, Friedrichstrasse, Frankfurt-am-Oder. Another border. Passengers alight and newcomers board. A little battered around the edges, the men hang up their leather jackets and pad the corridor in vests and tracksuit bottoms; the women in leggings and slippers. They offer me boiled potatoes and eggs from tinfoil wrappers. Their children crayon pictures. No one yells into their mobile phone. I sit on red plush and watch the flat Polish landscape unfurl through the length of the afternoon. Teaspoons chink against glasses set in silvery holders. Poznan, Warszawa Centralna, Warszawa Wschodnia.

A long wait while another train is coupled to ours. Again I pull out the book of letters.

The Germans were roaring terribly, the trams stopped, in the streets – darkness and filth. I live in one dark room. Two other rooms are uninhabited, they do not have blackout and in Nikita's room more than half the glass in the windows is broken and badly patched up with cardboard and paper. It is very cold in there...

Its author was a schoolteacher, Anna Alexeeva. Her daily ration was a quarter of a loaf of bread, half of it sawdust. Her electricity was cut off. She had to fetch water from an ice hole in the Fontanka river. Temperatures fell to minus forty degrees – the coldest winter in a hundred years. Nights were passed running to and from bomb shelters. On the streets trams, cars and pedestrians were ripped apart by shells.

The train lurches to a halt. The border between Poland and Belarus, once the western frontier of the USSR. We are shunted into the railway shed of Peace and Friendship. Metal clamps hoist our carriage while men scuttle about beneath changing the bogies (in the nineteenth-century, long before tanks were invented, the Russians built their railways on a wider gauge as a safeguard against invasion). Hours later we slide away across no man's land.

Through passport control, Brest station. The screech of wheels and female voices. Bleached heads bob alongside our window, racing towards the carriage door. Our compartment is invaded by pink lipstick smiles. Stout arms clutch home-baked pies, beer and sour milk. 'Kefir, sweetheart, chocolate, champagne…'

'Let me buy your kefir for you,' whispers a fellow passenger, a librarian from Omsk. 'Otherwise they'll cheat you. They will see you are foreign.'

Minsk, Smolensk. Dusk falls for the second night on the train. The carriage attendant warns us to fasten our compartment doors from the inside.

'What for?' I ask the librarian.

'As protection from bandits. They rob sleepers on international trains – sometimes they spray the car with gas. But don't worry, there should be armed guards on this train.'

Absurdly, this sounds romantic, an echo of civil war days of the 1920s. I lock the door.

25 December 1943: I leave home at 7.30 a.m. while it is still dark and return, or rather crawl home, at about 7.30 in the evening. I find the walk easier in the mornings but in the evenings I get breathless and have to stop and lean against the walls of buildings to rest for long periods. I stand in the darkness and think, 'This is the end.' Even if a shell explodes close by it makes no difference as I have not the strength to take another step, all I can do is close my eyes.

Yet Alexeeva found the strength to describe her hell. I switch off the overhead light and slide between the sheets of my narrow berth.

❦

The sun rises over rolling fields and tiny wooden Baba Yaga huts shrouded by silver birches. Seated on a vinyl banquette in the restaurant car I breakfast on rye bread and pickled cabbage. On the other side of the window tall grass, willowherb and ragwort line the tracks. A paper trail of white butterflies blows over the flowers. Lace curtains sway by my shoulder. The book of letters lies open by my plate:

Leningrad, 20 January 1945, Saturday, 12 midnight:
My dear Verochka,

At 10 p.m. a neighbour came by with a notice from the War Office. They have summoned me today at midday, 'Concerning the fate of your family member Nikita Vladimirovich Alexeev.'

So this summons lies here before me. You know yourself what people who receive such summonses can expect to hear. For two hours I paced like a pendulum from corner to corner. At first my leg began to drag itself suspiciously, but I used all my strength to try to pull myself together. There is no way I can die because I am too indebted to you (not only for the money but for that which is so much dearer than money).

Nikita and you, you and Nikita – you fill my thoughts. And here I sit writing to you, the only person left close to me in the world.

Notice

Your son Sergeant Alexeyev Nikita Vladimirovich of 53 Fontanka, flat 38, date of birth 1925

was killed on 11 October 1944 in the defence of the Socialist Motherland

All Anna Alexeeva had left of her son were his mud-covered boots retrieved by a soldier who had fought in his unit.

'May I join you?'

The man by my side has mild blue eyes and rotting teeth. He wears a crumpled shirt, shorts, grey socks and leather sandals. Unmistakably a compatriot.

Still reluctant for company, I glance around. The other tables are occupied.

'Please do.'

My new companion introduces himself as Harry from Portsmouth. 'I'm going to Japan. Looking for work. I'm a builder.'

'You're taking the Trans-Siberian?'

He nods.

'I've always wanted to do that.' And it's true. I've been many times to European Russia but never east of the Urals.

'You see so much from the train.' He pulls back the curtain at his side. Beyond the window three head-scarved women bounce across a ploughed field in a tractor-trailer.

'Where are they going?' my companion muses. 'Who is waiting for them?' He takes a swig from the glass of beer that the waitress has placed before him. 'England is predictable. You pass back gardens with people work-ing in them. You know there will be someone inside

8

getting the tea ready. Here you don't know anything. There is a whole world but people don't see it. They fly everywhere.'

He drains his glass. 'Nice talking to you.' He ambles out of the dining-car.

Later there is a knock at the door of my compartment. The carriage conductor stands before me, the philosopher-builder behind him.

'We have a small problem,' the conductor slurs. 'Tonight I want to show my friend Garry the sights of our beautiful Moscow.'

Harry beams. His eyes are unfocused.

'Unfortunately,' the conductor continues, 'I speak no English and Garry no Russian. Will you do us the honour of being our interpreter?'

Now I have to polish my number one Russian survival skill – the avoidance of drinking parties without giving offence. 'Nothing would afford me greater pleasure,' I reply, 'but I have a connection to St Petersburg.'

The conductor waves his hand. 'I can arrange for your ticket to be changed.' He taps his chest. 'I too have connections.'

'The problem is this.' I inject a note of regret into my voice. 'My friends in Petersburg have organised a reception for me. Tonight.'

I am making myself out to be the Wedding General,* but a white lie will allow the conductor to save face.

'Then you must go!' His heart will not withstand the guilt of spoiling someone else's party. 'Garry! Come with me. I have an idea…' He wraps his arm around Harry's shoulder and together they sway down the corridor.

---

* From the Chekhov play *The Wedding* where a general is invited in order to confer status on the hosts.

I alight in Moscow at the Belorusskii station. A woman drags the wheels of her trolley over my foot.

'Ouch.'

'Watch where you're fucking going.'

I take the circle line to Leningrad station. 'Mind the doors…' A shove in the back. 'Vanka, get your arse in.' A belly laugh. Red eyes glitter, arms drape over shoulders. Hungover *limitchiki,* male and female, migrants from the steppes granted precious residence permits now their labour is needed to build towers for the new Russian rich. Around us solemn Muscovites bury their heads in books and papers.

I share a compartment on the *Arrow* with a man and woman in their fifties. They chatter like excited children, rubbing shoulders as we rush through the night. Lovers? Russian affairs are conducted on long-distance trains. Flats are too cramped; there is no privacy. Yet this couple address each other by the formal 'you'. They are colleagues of thirty years, they tell me, engineers on a business trip.

We talk into the night. Why am I so interested in Russia they want to know? I tell them how my teenage reading – *War and Peace*, *The House of the Dead*, *Cancer Ward* – introduced me to the wider questions of life. At university I fell in love with the country's history, then with its language, music and poetry, and later still, although I don't mention this to my companions, with one of their compatriots.

Had I been to Petersburg before?

Twice, briefly, when it was Leningrad.

The engineers smile. How wonderful to be going now, independently like this, to see Petersburg myself.

Dawn breaks over crumbling factories and concrete housing blocks, a mirror of the city I left behind. *Pank's not dead* scrawled on a wall in English. Allotments, sidings, Kolpino, Petroslavyanka… A graveyard of rusting steam engines.

Lena is waiting on the platform with flowers.

2

…Scarcely able to breathe, I hurry to work
The sea-wind whipping my face
But the lictor strolls behind me*
And whispers, 'Memento mori.'
Anna Alexeeva, 5 February 1942

We exit the station carrying my bag between us. Lena and I have not seen each other for four years. It is a shock to notice white hairs among brown and the sharpened creases at the sides of her mouth. She is barely forty; she has three jobs. Like most people here, she cannot survive on one salary.

We first met in the Moscow Kremlin ten years ago, during my second visit to what was still the USSR. I had a private invitation from an Australian journalist who lived in a block just off the inner ring road. She obtained tickets to see Vasiliev's ballet *Macbeth* in the brutalist Palace of Soviets. I remember little of the performance

---

* Lictor – a magisterial bodyguard in ancient Rome who carried out the death sentence in time of war.

except to wonder at the orchestra playing *Greensleeves* during the murder scenes. I found one of our Russian companions more interesting – a thin, intense girl in long skirt and ankle boots, a pin-tucked shirt buttoned to her chin, who quizzed me on cockney rhyming slang during the interval. She said she was a native of St Petersburg – Leningrad as it was then – but was studying at Moscow State University.

Afterwards Lena took me to a bar at the Architects' Union. Members only but she had connections. The bar was one of the few places in the city where one could get a drink – this was a time of food rationing and dry laws. We sat in the faded splendour of the Union bar and I questioned her about her existence.

'It's not food I worry about; it's saving my soul.'

Uncertain how to respond, I summoned that rare sight – a passing waiter – and ordered another round of drinks.

In the days that followed Lena showed me around Moscow. The October revolution holiday was approaching. Grey facades were gashed by red; Lenin glared from street corners. I followed Lena through a snowy landscape into backstreet churches where headscarved women bowed and kissed icons in musky gloom.

Later, after the collapse of the Soviet Union, she visited me in London. She would skip her English classes to watch the changing of the guard. It was a metaphor for our way of life, she said.

And then in the summer of 1992 I went to stay in Samara. As a centre for the aviation industry and armaments production it had been closed to westerners since the Second World War. I wanted to see how people lived in the forbidden land of my childhood and youth. An invitation from a friend of Lena's secured me a visa.

I rented a hut in a holiday camp for chocolate factory

workers. Lena came to visit. We swam and walked through pine woods. I embarked on my book while she continued to wrestle with her faith. After she returned to St Petersburg I stayed on in Samara, renting a room in a *komunalka*, a communal flat in the old part of the city. A shop opened on the corner of my street selling imported western goods. I wandered in one day in search of a pen that did not leak. Ivan was standing behind the counter.

❦

I tire, the bag sags. Lena's thin arm takes up the slack. With her free hand she flags down a Lada. Its Tatar driver speeds terrifyingly along the rutted street where Dostoevsky once lived. Down Nevsky, past the Admiralty spire, we cross the sparkling Neva and head out to the suburb where Lena lives. The Tatar flirts. He wants to show the foreign lady around the city. Am I married? How many children? He kisses our hands when we give him some cash for the ride.

Lena's one-roomed flat is on a Soviet-era housing estate that looks like any other from Leipzig to Vladivostock. Grey concrete blocks file into the distance, fourteen storeys high, stained cliff faces in which families have built their nests, patching balconies with corrugated plastic, metal sheeting and tattered strips of tinfoil. Rooftops are spiked with TV aerials; linked by swathes of telephone wire. Inside, each block is the same as its neighbour: a metal security door opening onto a concrete stairwell smelling of rotting cabbage. Stray dogs doze behind hot water pipes. On the seventh floor Lena unlocks a gate, another security door, a padded front door and we are in her flat.

One large room, a kitchen, bathroom and balcony. Solid Soviet furniture made to last. In the kitchen a small table and four square stools. Nothing to distinguish it from any other flat. The wallpaper in the hall and kitchen is a shiny pebble-effect design, puffy to the touch; two contrasting green geometric patterns cover the living room walls. Yet the effect is faded, old-fashioned and pleasant, reminiscent of some English boarding-house of thirty years ago.

Lena opens a door off the kitchen. She shows me a room no larger than a cubicle containing an iron bedstead. The walls are lined from floor to ceiling with books. On the wide windowsill a stethoscope snakes around the largest collection of lipsticks I have seen outside a department store.

'This room belongs to my aunt. I came to live with her here last year. She insisted I had the main room while she lives in her cell, as she calls it. You'll meet her. She's away for the weekend, lecturing.'

'She's a doctor?'

'A specialist in children's illnesses. Officially she retired fifteen years ago but she took no notice. Come on, let's have lunch.'

Lena peels potatoes while I chop garlic and dill.

'How are you?' she asks. 'Have you written anything new?'

'No.' I was hoping to avoid this subject. I have been struggling for over a year now.

'I have been reading about the siege.'

Lena's knife works faster.

'Do they really know how many died?'

She sighs, lays down the knife and smoothes back a loose strand of hair. 'It was impossible to count. Perhaps half of us. We were three million before the war.'

Lena speaks as though she had lived through the

siege herself, when in reality it was lifted in 1944, fifteen years before her birth. Yet I understand her identification with her city's collective history. Although I was born in London more than a decade after the Second World War, I grew up believing I had only escaped the blitz by a whisker. Its legacy pervaded my childhood – in the talk of neighbours, in the gaping space between houses on the next street, in an aunt's terror as she cowered in her cellar during a thunderstorm.

'How did anyone survive?' I ask.

'Lake Ladoga froze over.' She pulls out a stool and sits down; her eyes distant. 'They opened a road across the ice to unoccupied Russia. It was called the Road of Life. Food was brought in but people went on dying. The supply trucks could not carry enough for the whole city. On the return journey they evacuated children.'

'I once knew someone who was evacuated across the Road of Life. She couldn't remember much about it.' Or perhaps she blocked it from her mind.

'German planes fired on them as they drove across the ice.'

'It must have been terrifying.' My finger prods at a wallpaper pebble. It is spongy beneath the plastic surface. I fight the urge to pick at it. 'Had they no cover?'

'Only blizzards. And then they got lost. They usually drove at night. They left the back of the truck open so people could jump if the truck started to go through the ice.

'There was food on the other side. But some people were unable to restrain themselves. They ate too much, too quickly, and died.'

'Such extreme conditions – how could anyone survive?'

She shrugs. 'They lived. They worked.'

'Wasn't there panic?'

'Not really. Don't forget we had the NKVD to

keep order. They shot people for rescuing sodden bags of flour from Ladoga. They called it looting.' She picks up her knife again. 'During the worst weeks non-manual workers were allocated 125 grammes of bread per day. People cut them into three thin slices – for breakfast, lunch and supper. And that's if they were lucky. On some days bread didn't appear in the shops at all. People were left holding their cardboard ration coupons.'

Three tiny slices – you would burn more energy than these provided by queuing in sub-zero temperatures to obtain them.

'Didn't they despair?'

She looks at me steadily. 'Yes. There was the psychosis of hunger.'

'Meaning?'

'At its worst, cannibalism. Murdering your children and eating them – for example.'

The kitchen is stifling. I drop the potato peeler and walk through a glass door onto the balcony. Below me children chase each other around a grassy courtyard, watched by head-scarved *babushki* sitting on benches in the shade of poplars. A folk tune drifts from a window in the opposite block. As if in response to the invisible accordionist a woman on a floor above bursts into song. '*Kalinka, Kalinka…*'

Another voice bawls at the singer, 'Turn it down!'

'Take a running jump!' the singer shouts back.

Across the main road a new apartment tower gleams pink and orange, twenty storeys high, all gloss and shine. *Pokazukha* – the Russian word for show and no soul. The tower is hideous, menacing even, the sort of building that eclipses its inhabitants, whereas here on the old estate the blocks are no more than a modest backdrop for the human life they contain.

Lena follows me onto the balcony. 'You didn't answer my question.'

'Which one?'

'About yourself. How are you?'

'Oh, fine.'

'What happened to that guy in Samara?'

'Ivan? That fizzled out.'

'Oh?' Her eyebrows lift.

'You knew already – I'm sure I told you. Anyway it was ages ago.' Turning away from her, I grip the balcony rail and lean over to watch a pack of dogs savage each other in the courtyard below.

As my train pulled in from Moscow I caught sight of him running along the platform, peering into the windows of each carriage. He carried a huge bunch of flowers. We spent a Dr Zhivago Christmas in a wooden *izba* rented from a beekeeper, sleeping curled up by the wood stove, beneath a roof weighed down by snow. When spring returned, with a blast of fierce Asiatic heat, we sailed on the Volga, stopping to bathe by sandy islets. Ivan spent hours explaining his life and his homeland to me; we were equally companions in silence.

One day after I had been there for a few months, Ivan asked me to take a drive with him. His mood was unusually serious. He stopped the car outside a newly-built block on the river bank. A man in army uniform hurried down the entrance steps to help me out of the car. He escorted us upstairs to a spacious flat, where he fell into a deep discussion with Ivan, leaving me to weave between glass-fronted cabinets and beige leather sofas to the balcony.

As we drove away Ivan asked what I thought of the place. I said it had a nice view. He told me he had made an offer on it. We would register ourselves, he said.

It took me a minute to realise this was a proposal.

His mother would do the housework as he understood I didn't care for it. He would work to support us; I could spend my days writing.

I panicked. For an afternoon I paced up and down the embankment beneath the prospective flat, trying to envisage an impossible future among the occasional tables and beige leather. On the far bank of the river wild steppe undulated in layers of blue and violet. I pictured myself sitting on the balcony like a captain on the bridge of a ship, watching the colours change with the light, day after day for the rest of my life.

An oil tanker sailed past, bound for the Caspian Sea. More than anything in the world, I wished I was on it.

The last I saw of Ivan was his tear-stained cheek pressed to the window of the *Seagull* express as it pulled out of Moscow's Kazan station. He raised his hand to the glass. I picked up my case and walked down to the circle line, as numb as frostbite.

※

'Let me tell you a story.' Lena rests her elbows on the balcony rail beside me. 'It's a love story – a real one.'

I'm not in the mood for love stories.

Lena reads my expression. 'You raised a question back there in the kitchen. I'm trying to answer it for you.'

Usually I enjoy her discursive speech, but today I'm impatient. I want straight answers, not fairy tales.

'Alexander Nikolaevich Boldyrev was an Orientalist who worked at the Hermitage Museum,' she begins. 'He fell in love with a young married woman, Victoria Garbuzova. One day he called at her home while her husband was out and made a declaration. She replied that she too had loved him for a long while. Then she sent him away. That evening she told her husband Alexander Paster about the visit. He asked what she wanted to do. "Nothing," she replied. "Alexander Nikolaevich has a family and I have – you."'

I peer over the balcony rail. Beneath us a group of men raise beer bottles to their mouths as they slide dominoes across a metal table. TV sets blare, pots clatter in unseen kitchens, frying meat and peppers scent the hot air.

'War broke out,' she continues. 'Volunteers were selected for the front, Boldyrev among them. Paster was a military commander. She went to him in tears. He said he would see what he could do.

'A few days later she was summoned by the director of the Hermitage, Joseph Orbeli. Before she could open her mouth Orbeli remarked that she had a wonderful husband.'

'I can imagine what most men would have done in his position.'

'What would have been the point of sending Boldyrev to almost certain death?' Lena's voice is sharp. 'It wouldn't have changed anything. Victoria's husband was too intelligent not to see that.'

'Intelligence and emotion do not always coincide.'

She glares at me. I am spoiling her story.

'Okay. What happened?'

'Shortly afterwards, without any explanation, Boldyrev was discharged from active service and sent home. Almost all the men in his regiment were killed at the front. Boldyrev stayed in the city throughout the siege, lecturing at the Hermitage. When the war ended he married Victoria.'

'What happened to Paster – did he survive too?'

'Yes. He died in 1987.'

Lena shows me the book in her hand. 'And this is the point of the story.' A hardback with a plain black cover, *A.N. Boldyrev, Siege Notes (Blockade Diary)* is engraved on it in gold lettering, like a tombstone.

'Boldyrev kept this diary throughout the siege. After his death Victoria prepared it for publication. It came out last year.

'I want to read you something from it. It made a great impression on me.' She flips through the pages. 'Here we are… Boldyrev had a friend whom he called Uncle Sasha, a professor of ancient languages, a gentle cultured man who never raised his voice. He describes how they met in a canteen for lunch one day. Uncle Sasha is distressed.' Peering short-sightedly at the text, Lena reads, '*Meat, there's no meat today,*' he said in an *impatient tone. 'No there isn't,' I said. 'They're giving us soya soup today.' 'Where's the meat?' he asked me almost rudely, fixing me with a strange, watchful stare.*

'When I read that,' says Lena, 'a voice within me cried out – that could have been me!'

Gripping my arm, she stares intently into my eyes. 'You asked what the psychosis of hunger was – well precisely that. It possessed people, transformed them.'

I twist my head away from her gaze, fixing my eyes on the tower across the road. It looms over the old estate, a silent reminder of the place where I might have lived.

'The spirit begins to die before the flesh,' she goes on. 'The ties that bind one to the rest of humanity are loosened. And then, well, who knows what people are capable of? Like poor Uncle Sasha, their speech changes; their vision alters. They might find a corpse in the street and see meat; they might find a living child and see meat…' Her voice catches. 'Damn, the kasha's burning.' She releases me and dashes back into the kitchen.

❧

The sky is milky, the sun has just dipped behind the tower block opposite ours. In this light it is hard to sleep. I roll onto my side and trace the pattern on my pillowcase: tiny blue flowers woven around the letters *Minzdrav*. A shortening of *Ministerstvo Zdravookhraneniya* – Ministry of Health – in the Orwellian language of the Soviet era. I imagine the Leningrad wounded lying in their hospital beds, tucked beneath pristine *Minzdrav* sheets.

Wide awake now, I get up and cross to Lena's desk where Boldyrev's diary lies open. I flick through the pages, my eyes settling on random entries. Obsessive records of food eaten – weighed to the gramme – and details of food collected on ration cards. There is work: chopping wood; reading a lecture: *In a vast basement room, by the light of hanging lamps, I spoke to a strange audience in dressing-gowns, head-coverings, bandages. Among the soldiers were elderly civilians, dystrophics, ragged hags with the spark of hunger in their eyes. The gloom was full of strange twisted figures, like a wild Rembrandt dream.*

Ivan once showed me an antique stereoscope he had acquired. I peeped through the view hole of the wooden box at anaglyphic Chekhov scenes. Girls in white dresses and picture hats played croquet, drank tea on a lawn with their governess, chased a little dog… With perfect focus, Boldyrev's diary zooms straight into the dark heart of the siege.

Scenes of disintegrating daily life: *There is no water in the entire city… Ice holes have been cut in the Neva, the rivers and canals. Endless lines go to and fro with buckets and vessels of all kinds. Factories are idle. They can't put out fires, houses burn like candles.*

Of civic duty – cleaning frozen shit from the streets: *The stench of liquefying chocolate snow is disgusting. When you dig into it with an axe and crowbar thousands of drop-lets spatter your face and clothes. I leave after an hour, falling over and pretending to have hurt my knee.*

Boldyrev's honesty is compelling. I take his diary to bed with me. It is light enough to read without disturbing Lena.

More scenes follow, of death in the streets: *I walked home beneath the dazzling frosty moon: on Chernyshevksy, between Sadovaya and Arkaya a person lay in the middle of the road. It seemed that he had only recently collapsed. Nobody stopped.*

His marriage fractures under intolerable pressure. His body starts to fail: *Now a difficult period begins, which means I shall have to write briefly – as in a crisis, like the final pages of the diary of a dying polar explorer: today there is no water and no bread.*

The struggle for life: *Today I didn't get up until 1 o'clock. Very weak. For the first time my face has swollen. Lying in bed my spirits fell, I experienced something like hysterics: i.e. I simply howled for a while… Death sucks one towards it like a current beneath a narrow bridge. As soon as you lower your guard you have to redouble your efforts to escape it.*

A few years ago I felt as though I was being sucked towards an unnameable menace. Beneath Ivan's nouveau riche lifestyle there flowed a more sinister current. Now, as I read about events that happened more than half a century ago, I feel the tentacles of the siege reach far into the future until they hook onto my own life.

Although it is a warm night I unroll the duvet and pull it up to my chin. I close Boldyrev's diary and lay it on the floor beneath my bed.

❦

'The diary caused a stir when it was published.' Lena plunges her hands into a sink full of last night's washing-up. 'It was such a wide departure from heroic siege myth. Boldyrev's widow wrote in the preface that reading it was so painful that she wondered whether it would have been better not to have asked her husband to intervene on his behalf, and to have let events take their course. She was wrong, of course. He has left us with a remarkable legacy.'

'Leave that, I'll do it. You'll be late.'

She goes off to work. I decide to spend the morning exploring her neighbourhood. I wander past housing blocks, a kindergarten, a clinic, a supermarket, *Pizzeria Cilantano*, shops offering western cosmetics and air conditioners. Finally I stop before a dusty window festooned with dying pot plants: *Souveniri.* Perhaps here… I push open the wooden door. The interior rattles with slot machines, rap music and teenage boys.

I am searching for ghosts, for shops where assistants doze behind abacuses, where glass counters display single treasures: a toothbrush, a plastic comb, a roll of grey toilet paper, a painted wooden spoon. And where the food is fresh and unprocessed: rye bread, nutty sunflower oil as thick as honey, and live yoghurt that is spooned into containers you provide yourself. Yet now these shops have almost disappeared, being replaced by supermarkets and Commission stores like the one Ivan owned.

He had begun his capitalist life working in a shop on the corner of the street where I lived in Samara. He sold pens, watches and leather jackets bought from Middle Eastern students, paying a percentage of his profits to the shop owner. By the time I returned he had amassed enough money to buy the shop himself and rent out counter space to other entrepreneurs.

He had a toy, a Coca-Cola tin that sang *Rock around the Clock* in a Donald Duck voice. He would visit his shop, place the tin on a counter and wind the key. As the tin began to writhe and sing a crowd of shoppers would gather around it, wide-eyed. I longed to knock that vile fetish object off the counter and crush it under my foot.

I reach the metro. Here I find a throng of *babushki,* their wares laid out on either side of its glass entrance. These old ladies have brought their home-grown produce to the city – honey, cream, fruit and vegetables. Once I took these women for granted; now I realise that the war generation is dying out, that soon no one will be bothered to grow their own food and transport it to the city. It is a tough, heavy way to earn a living. And many shoppers, particularly the young, prefer the speed and convenience of supermarkets.

I approach a vendor who is packing up. She tips her last jar of raspberries into my bag.

'Can I pull your trolley for you?'

'Just as far as the road. My son will meet me in his car.'

The woman shuffles beside me, fissured heels overhanging the backs of her slippers. A bouquet of flowers is laid on a plaque at the kerbside: black marble, gold lettering, a photo of a young man.

'Car accident?'

'Assassination.' She sighs, 'Things are changing around here.'

Being a *biznesmen* has its risks. I learned that much in Samara.

'Have you lived in this area long?'

'I am a native of this city. I grew up by the Fontanka.'

'May I ask if you lived through the siege?'

The woman surveys me through narrowed eyes. 'You are not a usual type of foreigner, I see.'

'Why do you say that?'

'Because you ask such a question.'

'I'm sorry.' Tactless of me.

'Not at all,' she replies. 'It was a very dark time. All sorts of things happened here. People stole from the flats of the dead, they stole ration cards from corpses, they... Well, but to answer your question, no. Just after war broke out I was evacuated with my parents. They were engineers at a defence plant. But my grandparents were left behind.' Her voice falters. 'They lived in a village to the west of Leningrad.'

'What happened to them?'

'They were shot by the Germans before they could escape. Suddenly it became important who was a Jew and who was not.'

She dabs her eyes with the sleeve of her overall. 'We came back after the war. I graduated and worked as an engineer. Now I am retired. I sell the fruit from my son's dacha. Here he is now.' She reaches for the handle of her trolley. 'It is quiet around here. Sometimes people move in from the country and make a bit of a row but on the whole we get along. Well, thank you. May God go with you.'

❧

According to the clock it is late evening. Lena's kitchen is flooded by sunlight. We sit drinking tea together.

'So how did anyone survive?' I ask.

'How does anyone survive?' Her voice sharpens. 'You just get on with it. One day follows the next. The *blokadniki* had to work, queue for rations, fetch water, drag corpses into piles…'

Her eyes narrow. 'Self-pity requires energy. They didn't have any to spare.'

It is almost a reproach. I try to imagine myself rising at three in the morning to join a queue of thousands outside the bakery, waiting for hours in minus 30 degree temperatures. And keeping my mouth shut throughout, because there will be informers ready to report the slightest grumble as counter-revolutionary defeatism. And going home empty-handed. I might as well imagine growing wings.

'But,' I persist, 'when your family, friends and neighbours are dying all around you, when your rations are cut below the minimum required to sustain human life, when daily life is disintegrating the way Boldyrev described, might you not just collapse? If I imagine myself in those circumstances I see myself succumbing pretty quickly.'

'You don't know until you are put to the test.' She whirls around to face me. 'Why don't you talk to some *blokadniki*?'

'Do you know any?'

'My mother was one. She survived the siege but it weakened her. She died while she was still quite young. I was in my teens.'

'*Scaramouche, scaramouche, can you do the fandango…*'

'God these walls are thin.'

'You get used to the noise.'

'I'm sorry. About your mother I mean.'

'That's all right.'

'You must have told me. I forgot.'

Lena shrugs. 'She didn't like to talk about it. She said it was best not to dig among the entrails.'

Ivan was also a second generation *blokadnik*. His mother Larisa had been orphaned during the siege and evacuated across the Road of Life.

'But her sister is very much alive,' Lena says. 'My Aunt Nadya. She'll be home later. She will talk to you.'

'I don't want to upset her.'

'She is not like my mother.'

'*Thunderbolt and lightning, very very frightening…*'

'Can we ask them to turn it down?'

'They'll go to bed in a minute. They get up for work at five. Talking of which…' She rises and carries her cup to the sink. 'It may be difficult for you but just remember, you have to maintain the vertical connection…'

Her words are lost in the flow of running water.

3

Petropolis is turning into a necropolis.
Nikolai Antsiferov – *The Soul of Petersburg*

A key turns in the front door and a tall woman in a mauve linen suit enters. Her eyes are blue and sharp in a flat, almost Tatar face. White hair springs from a high forehead; her mouth is a vivid slash of orange. Her presence makes the flat feel suddenly cramped. She extends her hand. 'Nadezhda Ivanovna. Welcome.' Her grip is painful.

She kisses Lena, pulls off her outdoor shoes and walks through into the kitchen. We follow.

'We have been talking about the siege.' Lena pours three glasses of tea from a pot that has been stewing on the samovar and tops them up with fresh water.

'Oh yes?' Aunt Nadya regards me more closely. I lower my eyes, feeling like a guilty twelve-year-old being scrutinised by her headmistress.

'She wants to know what it was like,' says Lena.

I draw a deep breath. 'If you don't mind.'

'I'll tell you.' Taking a gulp of tea, Aunt Nadya puts

down her glass. 'But now you'll have to excuse me. I must write up my notes before I go to bed. Be ready by nine o'clock tomorrow morning. Wear walking shoes.'

Her cell door shuts with a click.

❧

'The building on our right is the Academy of Fine Arts, built in 1757...' Aunt Nadya maintains a running commentary as our tram crosses the Neva to Vasilievsky Island. The torrent of words washes over me while my eyes follow a row of neglected tenements. We are in Gavan, the city's port district. A sign *Our Factory – Our Pride!* rusts above rooftops. We pass a brutalist concrete terminal to which ferries no longer run, round a bend in the road and stop beside a row of black metal railings with spear tips. 'This is the Smolensk Cemetery. Its chapel is dedicated to Ksenia the Blessed, saint of the city.'

We alight and follow a path shaded by birches and pines. The resin-scented air is clouded with poplar down. Blue speedwell peeps from beneath foliage. We reach the chapel to find it crowded with hopeful girls in stilettos and puffs of bleached hair, nouveaux riches in Versace and stout housewives from Gavan. They bend over pens and slips of paper and then hand their written prayers to a bearded priest – the only man in the building.

'They believe he will intercede for them with the Blessed Ksenia.' Aunt Nadya's voice booms around the walls of the little chapel.

Scarved heads nod and bow before icons like poppies in the wind.

I feel as though I am watching the scene from a far distant place. The spirit of Lena leans over my shoulder, urging me to peer over the wall of my western rationalism.

'Who was Ksenia?' I ask.

'An eighteenth-century noblewoman. She was only twenty-six when her husband died during a drinking session. Alcohol poisoning.' Aunt Nadya sniffs. 'He died before he had confessed his sins and this upset Ksenia so much that she declared herself to be dead. She took on her husband's identity and became what was known as a Holy Fool, following the Russian tradition of giving away all her possessions and wandering the streets as a beggar.'

An old beggar woman I once met on some church steps in Samara told me there is a finite amount of evil in this world. Taking an extra portion on one's shoulders will lighten the burden of another.

'Whatever Ksenia received she gave away. People believed that if they gave to her then good fortune would befall them; if they refused, misfortune would follow. Market traders were especially generous.

'She helped to build that church over there.' Aunt Nadya points to a dome rising above treetops. 'At night she would load materials onto her back, climb a ladder the builders had left behind and continue with the work. The Blessed Ksenia is considered a role model for women.' She lets out a bark of laughter.

Outside, women surround the little chapel, kissing its blue-washed walls and muttering prayers. Behind them, male drunks shuffle beneath the shelter of bushes. When a woman peels away from the wall they approach on unsteady legs and beg softly for money.

'Wait here a minute.' Aunt Nadya strides over to a man on crutches and presses a note into his hand. They exchange a few words.

'He used to work in our faculty of medicine,' she tells

me as we walk away. 'A heart specialist. Drank away everything. His wife left him. The usual story.'

Bidding me follow her, Aunt Nadya weaves her way between overgrown graves to a tall silver birch. 'I did fire watch duty here.'

It is a lonely spot.

'Weren't you afraid to spend the night here? You were only a teenager.'

She shakes her head. 'No. Perhaps I had so little fear because I was young and anxious to play my part.' She pauses to consider for a moment. 'And I am not talking about Hitler versus Stalin as they make out in the propaganda. We were fighting for our own lives and for each other's.' She strokes the white birch trunk beside her. Slivers of bark curl back to reveal tender spots beneath.

'And we were so protective of our city. In the middle of September 1941, when we were fully expecting a German invasion, they prepared to dynamite the main buildings: the Kirov works; railway bridges; factories and so on. But not the palaces, not Peterhof, Pavlovsk nor Tsarskoe Selo. They removed the machine guns from the roof of the Winter Palace – the Hermitage – in order not to give the Germans an excuse for attacking it.

'Although we were freezing we would not cut down our trees for firewood. We resisted that. In spring 1942 we ate leaf buds, chewed pine twigs, boiled their needles. They are rich in vitamin C. Important for preventing scurvy.' She wraps her arm around the birch. 'This tree sheltered me. I would go off to sleep right here, using my gas-mask case as a pillow.'

Pulling a copy of *Izvestiya* from her briefcase, she separates the sheets and lays them on the ground. 'Sit down.' She leans back against the tree trunk and crosses her outstretched legs.

'I once knew someone who was orphaned in the siege,' I say, remembering Ivan's mother, Larisa. 'Do you still dream about it?'

'Of course. It would be strange if I didn't. I don't want to forget; the siege shaped my whole life.' Her blue eyes seem to bore through me. 'You know, when you see what human beings are capable of, when you have known the extremes, life holds very few terrors.'

She exhales a stream of smoke and raises her eyes towards the dome of the Smolensk church. 'In a way it was easier for our generation. We knew what we were up against. During the siege you had a stark choice. You did what you could to survive, because if not, you knew very well that outside there were thieves and cannibals. Perhaps they had once been your neighbours, pleasant, hard-working, apparently normal people. You saw what you could become, you saw what hunger did.'

'What does it feel like – starvation, I mean?' The question seems intrusive, but I want to try to imagine it from within, as it were.

Aunt Nadya pauses for a second. 'Many people wrote diaries during the siege.'

'I've been reading one.'

'Helped keep them alive. Lidiya Ginzberg – she was a literary critic – wrote in hers that hunger produces an alienation of the body. She described it as "an emaciated envelope with a soul located separately, somewhere inside the ribcage." And that is how it felt. Your body didn't want to work properly; it ignored commands. You felt as though you were nothing but mind, or will, if you like, striving to exert control over your reluctant, disobedient carcass. Ginzberg wrote that if you let go, the body would slither out of control and fall like a sack into some incomprehensible abyss.'

'As when one is seriously ill, perhaps?'

'We were seriously ill.'

'And the mind?'

'Well, the mind, will, soul, whatever you like to call it – that was another matter. If you allowed *that* to slither out of control along with your deteriorating physical body, then you were lost. That was the state we called moral dystrophy, the incomprehensible abyss in which people were capable of anything, anything at all.'

She stubs out her cigarette and throws the end into a bush. 'Come on,' she pulls me to my feet. 'We have a full programme today.'

4

Put on your white dresses… Lie down in your
coffins, prepare for death.
German leaflets addressed to the women
of Leningrad, dropped during autumn 1941

Stopping at a flower stall on Nevsky Prospect, I deliber-
ate over bouquets. 'For a ballerina,' I tell the vendor.

'Then take roses.'

'They have no scent.'

'Hothouse. What do you expect?'

I pay and walk along to an art nouveau building beside
the Philarmonia. My instructions are to press 4579 with
both hands while kicking open the door. Juggling the
roses as I perform this feat, I pass into an apartment
block of faded elegance. Stairs curve around a lift cage
threaded with wrought iron lilies.

'Who's there?'

The door opens a crack; I thrust the bouquet towards it.

'For me?' A tiny blonde woman stands on the threshold. Her eyes widen but her hands have already extended
towards the flowers.

Lena has used her connections to secure an invitation from this former prima ballerina with the Kirov, as the Marinskii was called in Soviet days. Nonna Borisovna Yastrebova ushers me into a sitting-room shaded by blinds. It is unlike any I have seen in the city, full of antique sofas, tables and lamps. A rare sight in Petersburg; most old furniture was used as firewood during the siege.

Nonna glides across the room to a divan. She sits erect, her narrow waist emphasised by the tightly drawn belt of her trouser suit. I slump in a velvet armchair. Facing her, I recall a woman who sat with equal poise on a hard chair in her one-room flat in an industrial suburb of Samara. Ivan's mother Larisa had been a few years younger than Nonna when war broke out. They lived only a few streets away from each other, yet their fates turned out very differently.

'It was 22 June 1941.' Nonna's voice rings out as though she were on stage. 'I walked to rehearsal through streets bathed in sunlight. At the theatre I started to warm up. Bliss flooded my limbs.'

I feel as if she had taken my hand and pulled me into the Kirov with her.

'During the interval someone called me over to the radio. Molotov's voice: "Brothers and sisters..." An unusual form of address. We sensed something serious was taking place. "At 4 a.m., without declaration of war, German troops attacked our country."' Her voice fades to a whisper.

'Oh, I thought to myself, we shall have to cover the windows and not stay out too late. We had lived through the Finnish war of the previous winter. But then I saw that some of the older women in the theatre – the hairdressers and fitters – had begun to cry. One had a husband, another a brother... I continued to rehearse but the joy had gone from the day.

'A few days later the theatre held a dinner at the Astoria Hotel. The band began to play the hit song of that summer, *We'll Meet Again in Lvov, My Love and I*. My friends and I got up to dance. In a quiet voice the manager asked us to sit down. But we could barely contain ourselves. Later I twirled and danced by the river with the male members of the *corps de ballet*. The Neva sparkled in that white night. That was the last time I saw those boys.'

Noises float up from the street below. A curse, a screech of tyres. 'Hush!' I want to call out, as though someone were coughing in the auditorium.

'The theatre was evacuated. On the morning of 19 August I went to the station and saw off my friends. I wanted to leave with them but my aunt was too ill to move. I lived at home with her and my mother.'

'And your father – was he at the front?'

'What?' Nonna gives a start. 'My father… No, he was arrested and shot. In 1937. I don't know what for.'

Her hands fly up to brush away tears. 'Rations are cut again and again. We starve. There is no heating, no water, the sewage system breaks down, our flour is made from ground tree bark. Temperatures fall to minus forty degrees. The city is glassed over with ice; when a bomb falls it rattles like a crate of beer. We are constantly running down to the air raid shelter. We sit, old people, children, everyone hushed, the walls around us shaking from explosions.'

Nonna shudders. 'I take an elderly neighbour to hospital. He has no family and he thinks at least he will be fed there – they might have soup perhaps, and bread. He sits on my sledge and I pull him; he no longer weighs anything at all. As we approach the hospital we hear a terrible noise. Wooh! Woo-ooh! Like the howling of wolves.' Nonna's mascaraed blue eyes widen in terror. 'We draw closer.' She lowers her voice to a whisper. 'Starving, abandoned people stand at the windows, their hands pressed to the glass. Outside the hospital is a pile of corpses: blue, black, old, young, frozen people. They are twisted, grotesque. It is clear that those inside will soon join the heap in the yard. The hospital has no food. I turn and drag my neighbour home again.'

Sunlight silvers the tear tracks on Nonna's cheeks. 'One day there is a knock at the door. A cheerful voice calls, "Are you alive?" It is my former dancing partner, Misha Vorobyov. "What are you doing here dying of hunger? Come to us, join the army ensemble." My mother begs me not to leave. She is scared; her sister is dying. I go nonetheless, promising to do what I can to help her.

'A military car drives me to an army base in a beautiful colonnaded mansion. The barracks fill with philosophers, musicians and actors – I see Cherkassov.'

One of the greatest Soviet actors – immortalised by Eisenstein as Ivan the Terrible.

'I join a concert brigade. Our director is Georgi Nosov, the composer. He is strict: "You are serving in the Red Army; you will be under Red Army discipline." They set me to peeling potatoes. My fingers are numb; the bucket is huge. I despair. Then I feel two arms around me, lifting me up onto the counter. "Hup! Okay Nonna, let's get to work!" Arkadii the handsome trumpet player with lacquered hair has come to help me – along with the tall blond Strzhelchik – later he plays Napoleon in *War and Peace*.

'Our brigade is sent to the front. Two lorries are parked in a clearing, their open backs joined together. It is very cold and our "stage" is slippery after being hosed down. I am afraid of falling and breaking a leg – I have to dance on my *pointes*. Gluck's music begins to play.'

Nonna flutters her hands in time to inaudible notes. 'We fly through the air like rose petals in our green tunics. The soldiers watch us wide-eyed. They have never seen ballet before. When the dance ends they are too stunned to clap.'

She curls forward in a low bow, arms encircled before her.

'A young soldier approaches me and thrusts a bunch of wild grasses into my hands. "For you," he mumbles, blushing. He has wrapped some aluminium wire around the stalks.

Oh! I thank him. "My first bouquet!"

'After the performance those boys charge off into battle crying, "Forward! For *our* girls!"

'So you see,' says Nonna Borisovna as she returns to herself. 'People need not only bread and porridge, but also music and dance.'

She stretches out to clasp her ankles.

'For years I resented the war. It held back my career. All the porridge I ate at the front made me chubby.'

It can't have done too much harm, I think. She was prima ballerina at the Kirov until 1963. A star in the USSR while Larisa grew up to become a trapeze artist.

When Larisa was eight years old she was pulled alive from the basement shelter of her home. It had received a direct hit. She was scarcely injured. Her parents were killed.

Nonna's daughter-in-law Ira serves tea in the kitchen. Ira says her mother is a historian and these days they are discussing whether the city should have surrendered in 1941.

I am startled by this heresy, once punishable by execution.

'Perhaps. There might have been fewer deaths,' says Nonna.

'I don't think you even had a choice,' I say, 'because Hitler had ordered Leningrad to be razed from the face of the earth*. He refused to accept surrender.'

Ira nods. 'The Nazis would have shot everyone or let them all starve to death.'

After tea Nonna and I say our farewells.

'Be careful on the stairs. Robbers lurk in entrance-ways.' She sighs, 'Oh, how times have changed. I was born in this building. I have always loved Nevsky but you never see a cultured face on it now. Only in the Philarmonia – look at the faces in the Philarmonia. There you will still see the intelligentsia.'

I walk home in a daze, scarcely aware of the jostle of evening crowds. It has been a while since I thought about Larisa. When Ivan first took me to meet her she received me graciously, dressed in velvet, her hair bleached and waved, a white Persian cat on her knee. She bade me come closer. I stood beside her as her hands began to play around the dress I was wearing, studying its seams and darts. Abruptly she ordered me to undress. Tipping the cat off her knee, she went over to her wardrobe, the only piece of furniture in the room apart from a narrow bed, table and chairs. She pulled out a piece of blue satin and wrapped it around me. 'This will suit you better,' she said. 'Have it made up by your dressmaker.' As we left she turned a handstand in the corner of the room. She practised every day, Ivan told me. Like Nonna, she loved the stage too.

Ivan's father, an alcoholic, had left when he was six months old. Larisa had lost her job with the circus and gone to work in a missile plant. The woman's hostel where she was housed would not accept children. She had put him in the same home where she had grown

---

*   See Appendix 1

up, the one to which she had been taken after she was evacuated from Leningrad.

There was constant hunger in that home, he said. The staff sold off the supplies; bigger kids stole his food. But he had felt luckier than most of the other children, for he had a mother who came to visit him on weekends.

I reach the flat exhausted. Dropping my shopping on the kitchen table, I go to lie down on the sofa-bed. In a minute I will start to prepare supper for Lena's return. We have seen very little of each other over the past few days. She leaves early and returns late, too tired for conversation.

Music drifts across from the opposite block of flats. The invisible accordionist again. I close my eyes. Before me is a pine forest. In a clearing stands a truck with an open back. Rows of soldiers are seated on the ground, mere boys, their eyes shining in anticipation. Larisa swings from a high trapeze, the audience gasps.

I am awakened by Lena returning from her third job of the day.

'Lena! I'm so sorry. I meant to cook supper but I fell asleep instead.'

'It doesn't matter.' She sits down beside me. 'Did you meet Yastrebova?'

'I was privileged. She gave a private performance.'

I remember the conversation in the kitchen. 'Nonna's daughter-in-law told me that historians are now discussing whether Leningrad should have surrendered.'

'It was not an option.' Lena sighs. 'You see, it is fashionable now among certain sections of the intelligentsia to compare fascism with Communism. Only they say Communism is worse; it killed more people.'

'Well, it's true the *blokadniki* were caught between the twin evils of Stalin and Hitler...'

She shakes her head. 'That's not the point. In reality

the city was fighting for itself. For life, love, joy, art, music, humanity...'

'That's what your aunt told me.' I yawn. 'What I don't understand, though, is why I feel so tired. Compared to you I lead a life of ease yet all I want to do is sleep.'

'You are forgetting something.' Lena throws me a look of patience being tried.

'Oh?'

'The mind and body are not separate. You need to free yourself from that illusion.'

5

You used to say 'We are made of stone.'
No,
We are stronger than stone,
We are alive.
Margarita Aliger – *Spring in Leningrad* 1942

Tram number 29 rattles through southern suburbs towards the city's perimeter. The streets are wider here, where the city has sprawled beyond its wartime confines. Five-storey brick 'Khrushchev' blocks line the boulevards. We halt beside an overgrown park. Ravens tumble and dive over the trees like the Yaks and Messerschmitts which once fought in this sky.

'You must pray for forgiveness and God will hear you…' Across the aisle a fragile blonde girl is talking to a man crumpled with drink. Her bare face renders her striking in a city where girls prepare for work as though for a nightclub.

'… he forgives all our sins.'

The girl's sweet voice murmurs on while my eyes drift over dusty trees and shop fronts.

Lena's no different from this evangelist, I think to myself. A bit more sophisticated, that's all. I am still annoyed with her for patronising me.

The blonde girl alights.

'She's a good girl,' the drunk slurs to an old woman seated next to me. 'A believer.'

Even the drunks are more charitable than I. It must be the heat.

We pass a huge granite obelisk, the monument to Victory. Beside it is an advertising hoarding of a young man staring into an air hostess's half-opened blouse. *West cigarettes – everything is possible.*

My spirits plummet.

Arkadii Kotlyarsky is waiting at the tram stop. He wears dark glasses and an immaculately-pressed white shirt and trousers. A water melon is wedged under his left arm. He holds out his free hand to help me down from the tram. We stroll along a path shaded by silver birches.

'And how is Nonna Borisovna?' he asks. 'We are old friends from front-line days.'

'She seemed well, despite this heat. She is about to go to their dacha.'

He smiles. 'It was she, more than anyone else, who lifted the forces' morale. She was their sweetheart, the flower of the battlefield.'

Every passer-by stops to greet Arkadii.

'Arkadii Semeyonich, how are you?'

'Very well.'

'How is your wife?'

'In good health, too.'

'Praise be.'

'Would you like an ice cream?' Arkadii buys two and hands one to me. 'So you want to know how we survived the siege?' He licks his cone. 'Well, above all you had to preserve your humanity…'

'Arkadii Semeyonich, how much did you pay for that melon?' a red-faced woman calls out from an open window.

'Nine.'

'Nine! The robbers!' Her window slams shut.

'... And your humanity is closely connected to your creativity.'

The reminder stings. 'I'll give you an example,' Arkadii continues, 'I was performing at the front during the siege, singing couplets to celebrate Tank Drivers' Day. As I stepped off the stage Nonna handed me a letter. It informed me that my mother had died.'

Arkadii stops still in his tracks, vanilla ice cream dripping onto the path. 'Nonna had waited for that moment when she knew I was still under the spell of my performance, so that the blow was cushioned.' He clears his throat. 'A small gesture if you like, but it shows how sensitive she is.' He pulls out a handkerchief from his breast pocket and wipes his hands.

We enter an apartment block and climb four flights of stairs. 'Come out onto the balcony – feel how fresh the air is. I have been sleeping here on these hot nights.'

Below us female work gangs clear undergrowth from beneath silver birches.

'They work all day in thirty degree temperatures. I don't know how they do it.'

Arkadii's wife Bella prepares lunch in the tiny kitchen. They married after the war and worked in the circus together. 'No medals can compensate us Leningraders for what we lived through. You passed that monument to Victory on the way here? Well, that doesn't move me at all. But my experiences affect me to this day. I've heard the radio announcer, freezing and exhausted; I've seen the Musical Comedy actors, freezing and exhausted. Yet they carried on. And we watched them. Nothing would stop us going to the theatre.' Bella pauses, knife in hand, to wipe the sweat from her brow. 'Once I came out from a performance just as a shell fell on a passing tram. A stranger threw himself on top of me. He was cut by flying glass but we survived. That is the sort of heroism I remember.'

She slices the water melon, arranging sections on a dish. 'Hunger numbed the fear of bombing and shelling. It overrode everything; there was little room for anything else. People became so weakened that they would step on the corpses that lay half-buried in the snow rather than take an extra step to walk around them. We didn't have the strength.'

We sit down to a lunch of stuffed marrow and salad. While we eat Arkadii plays a tape.

'Moon and stars above me
I stand at the window and wait for you.
In the peace of this evening hour
I can't believe that you will not return.'

A Vera Lynn voice; 1940s dance band music.

'Klaudia Shulzhenko,' says Bella. 'I saw her once, on Women's Day – 8 March. She had come straight from the front to sing to us. She was still wearing army trousers. When she sang *Blue Kerchief* I sobbed and howled. There in the House of Army Officers we were celebrating life, while on the other side of those walls people were freezing, starving and dying. And after the concert, that is where I would return.'

'That winter of 1941–2 was hard,' says Arkadii. 'We couldn't survive on hot water with one lentil floating in it so our director sent us to the front where rations were slightly better. Even so, the sergeant-major went around every half hour to check that everyone was still alive.

'When I received my ration I would think if only it were a bit bigger then I'd be a happy man. After the war

I could not sleep unless I had a piece of bread under my pillow.'

Larisa was unable to sleep without a fridge full of food. That fridge occupied half her kitchen. Once I opened it and found chicken breasts, fruit, caviar and fresh fish, bought by Ivan. Larisa confided in me that she ate only sausage, black bread, potatoes and pickled cabbage. The rest she fed to her cat. Ivan called it the mentality of poverty; I had not connected it with the siege then.

'In spring the situation eased a little. We drank the sap of birch trees.'

And now I am back on a hillside overlooking the Volga. An early spring day, the snow melting, crows raucous overhead. Ivan taps a nail into the bark of a silver birch. We collect the sap as it drips from the wound he has made.

That sweet and cold taste is on my tongue, as raw and alive as the stalks of young grass but more delicate.

'The funny thing is,' I say, 'the sap of each tree tastes different.'

'And why not?' asks Arkadii. 'Doesn't each melon have a different flavour?'

Bella clears the table while Arkadii bursts into song:
'Oh you beautiful song; oh you song of my soul
Too lovely to be loved, by the fascist foe
'I was always trying to think up new couplets, new jokes. At one of our concerts on Kronstadt I saw a captain of the first rank break down and cry when we sang *Bezkazirka*. It was so moving to see that officer cry – that was the sort of emotional state we were in.'

Arkadii attempts to sing *Vyborg Side* but his voice falters. 'I am sorry. I am an actor and very emotional. Art is connected with the emotions. If it is not, then it is not art.

'We also played in children's homes. So many children had been orphaned by the hunger and shelling. The kids ran towards me crying: "Papa! Papa!"' Tears course down his cheeks.

'Entertainment is an exchange between you and your audience,' says Bella.

'It is the very breath of life to an actor, poet, or musician.' Arkadii recovers himself. 'When you entertain people who are far from home they welcome you as though you were a member of their own family. The gratitude of those troops overwhelmed me. When you go out hungry in front of a thousand soldiers they revive you. Their gratitude kept me alive.'

'They breathe life into you,' says Bella, 'then you forget your hunger.'

'And in return you give them… well you infect them,' says Arkadii. 'You see them change, their eyes come to life as they watch you.

'I'll never forget the first time I saw women with clean hands. Leningrad women… It was 1943 and I was playing in the Kirov tank plant. I hadn't seen manicured nails for a long time. They had made such an effort to clean their blackened hands for us. Oh, excuse me…' He wipes his eyes.

'In war,' he continues, 'it is the emotions that propel a soldier into battle. He doesn't command himself in a conscious way; the desire to defend your country is not based on rational thought. The soldier prepares for battle thinking that he could die, but when someone performs a concert in front of him he forgets his fear. He also forgets that his home might have burned down and his family been killed by bombs. Like an illusionist, you direct his attention away from his thoughts, he stops thinking about what might happen, whether he will survive until the next day, for his emotions are caught in the present moment. In this way you inspire him to go on living and fighting.

'So, in answer to your question, that is the Muse that would not be silenced. Oh, excuse me…'

Arkadii presses the handkerchief to his face again.

'Our lives changed after the war,' says Bella. 'Under Zhdanov's fight against cosmopolitanism, I was forbidden to play the saxophone.'*

'Why?'

'It was considered non-Russian,' Arkadii replies. "Only one step from a saxophone to a Finnish knife,' they said. So I went to the Leningrad circus. I became a musical clown, a new art form for me.'

He opens a drawer and sifts through a sheaf of photographs. 'Now look at this. It is a picture of Bella and me in our circus days.'

Arkadii holds a trumpet with one hand; his other is around Bella, striking in sequins, black hair flowing to her waist.

Larisa still mourned her days at the circus, her costumes, the applause. Her wardrobe was full of evening dresses and shoes. She said she bought them for the theatre. Ivan told me she had not been for twenty years.

'We travelled around the country,' says Arkadii. 'We played in prison camps.'

'It was frightening at first,' says Bella, 'but when we saw the convicts, murderers, whoever they were, running to greet us, we learned not to be afraid. They had such eagerness on their faces.'

'They gave us hope,' says Arkadii, 'for we understood by then that it is people without imagination who are the most capable of cruelty.'

---

*   See appendix on the Zhdanovshchina

6

…But not for anything would I exchange
This magnificent granite city of glory and tears
Of wide rivers of shining ice
And sunless, gloomy gardens
Where the voice of the Muse is barely heard…
Anna Akhmatova

'Most of us reach a point where we have to chose between life and death.' Lena gazes at the tomb at our feet. 'If we don't then perhaps we have not experienced life, certainly not enough to truly value it.'

'So what happened?'

We are visiting the poet Anna Akhmatova's grave at Komarovo, a settlement north of Petersburg where she had a summer house. A few bouquets rest against an ugly stone monument displaying a bas-relief profile.

Lena stoops to straighten a wilted flower in a cellophane wrapper.

'The winter before last I lost my job. The publisher I was working for was privatised and they wanted younger girls in shorter skirts.'

'That's stupid.'

She shrugs. 'It's the way things are these days. The only job I could find was selling detective novels on the street.'

'In winter?'

'Minus twenty. I worked beside a former naval officer and an architect who had taken to drink. Our employer was a young businessman with a ponytail.' She gives a wry smile. 'He had barely finished school and liked to have 'educated people' working under him.'

'How did you cope?'

'In those temperatures my organism seemed to shut down. I no longer thought of food. I met a soldier who said the same thing happened to him in Chechnya. He even lost the desire to smoke.'

Lena photographs me beside Akhmatova's grave. We walk away through a pine forest, our feet buoyed by springy moss.

'I would go home at night,' she continues, 'to a communal flat full of drunks. I had no energy for music, for reading. I started to take a bottle of vodka to work with me – to keep out the cold, or so I told myself. It was a very dangerous state to be in.'

The trees thin out. We reach a lake. Four-wheel drives with blackened windows are parked along the shore. Glass crunches underfoot.

'The new Petersburg rich have built their dachas out here.'

Sunbathers lie on a strip of sand. A young woman sits smoking on a towel. I have seen her face on mediaeval church frescoes, a fragile Slavic beauty, eyes like water and the softest of mouths. Her tiny black bikini has a red-fringe trim with a rose between her breasts. Around her is a tidemark of cigarette butts, plastic bags and beer bottles. She drops another bottle onto the sand. Beside her a transistor radio blares Russian pop music.

This crowd look like the kind of people Ivan used to do business with. At first I thought he arranged the bathhouse parties and boat trips through sheer enjoyment of the company. When I turned down a dinner invitation from some young entrepreneurs he was puzzled and asked what was wrong. I told him I had no interest in Emirates shopping sprees. I did not care what toys anyone had bought in the Gulf, still less how much they cost. Ivan had burst out laughing then. I did not understand the Russian way of doing business, he said. These people were his clients. He was building trust and connections, all the better to cheat them. He said this with such innocence that I laughed too, but I still declined the invitations.

Lena and I sit down at the water's edge. Had Ivan not gone into business he would probably have faced a life very similar to the one she has just described.

'I had no idea,' I say. 'How did you escape?'

Her fingertips dig into the sand. 'Aunt Nadya found me. Of course she recognised the symptoms straight away.'

'Symptoms?'

Her eyes flash. 'The siege. You see, the edge of despair is real. Like a cliff face, once you step over it, it is too late. Virtually no one returns. Aunt Nadya has seen it happen so often that she recognised the danger signs and took me in. Then she set to work on me. I have no doubt she saved my life.' Lena smiles. 'But it disappoints her that I went back to my orthodox faith. She is an atheist of course.'

A young man circles his jet ski towards the shore and revs the engine. When he has the attention of the girl on the towel he waves. She turns away with a pout, rolls onto her belly and lights another cigarette.

'We adapt to each other – I am very fond of her,' Lena continues. 'She is Soviet to the core: utterly selfless and at the same time deeply authoritarian.' She laughs out loud. 'I would never dare tell her that.' She stands up. 'Let's hire a rowing boat and get away from here.'

We walk down to a little jetty. The boat man wants to see our passports but we have not brought them with us. Neither of us drive and without documentation we can't hire a boat.

Behind us the jet ski roars. Sweat prickles my neck.

Lena steps forward. 'Well this is a shame. My friend here has come all the way from England. It would be a pity for her to go back without rowing on our beautiful lake.'

He beams. 'But why didn't you say so? My son is working in Germany.'

The man helps me into the boat. I take the oars and pull away, crunching over snail shells thrown up by a shore side dredger. They beat against the boat's hull like hailstones. And then the silence of clear water. My oars dip into a reflected sky of grey and white cumuli.

'Like the Egyptian dead, rowing to the afterlife.'

'Watch out,' says Lena.

Over my shoulder the hull of a motor boat looms, bearing down on us, keeping a straight course. I heave my right oar and we veer aside just as the boat passes. Its wash towers over our gunwale. We tilt and hang suspended. The wave passes and our boat bobs upright again. A young man in shades stands at the controls of his launch, laughing back at us as we rock in its wash.

'He's probably drunk,' says Lena, clutching the side of our boat.

I am shaken. 'That was so dangerous.'

'What does he care? He is above the law.'

The train back to the city is crowded with dusty city

folk returning from their dachas, hauling garden tools and sacks of cherries. Hawkers push their way through the aisles, offering sticking plasters, pens and magazines. Lena remarks to me in English, 'You attract a lot of attention. You don't know it but you do. Our fellow passengers are muttering that foreigners even ride on these trains.'

'Why wouldn't I?'

'They think it is too scruffy for you. They believe foreigners should only see what is best in our country.'

I smile at her. 'I'm talking to the *blokadniki*.'

7

*The Haymarket was the centre of trade in flesh, as in
every kind of food product...*
Harrison Salisbury, *900 Days: The Siege of Leningrad*

Gypsy children dart into the traffic, thrusting upturned
palms through the open windows of cars stopped at
the lights. A woman in a flowered headscarf sits nursing
a baby in the shadow of the walls of the eighteenth-
century Anichkov Palace. Ignoring her outstretched
hand I enter the grounds through ornate iron gates.
Aunt Nadya has given me a letter of introduction but
the receptionist is dubious. 'Who are you and where is
your authorisation?'

She phones to check. My clothes and accent tell her
I am foreign and she has been trained to be vigilant.
Frowning, she puts down the receiver and mumbles,
'Room 45.'

A curved staircase leads up to spacious landing hung
with children's paintings. This Palace was built by Peter
the Great's daughter, the Empress Elizabeth, but since
1934 it has been dedicated to children. They come after

school to practise music and sport, to paint and dance. For a short while at the start of the siege it was turned into a hospital for wounded soldiers. Aunt Nadya told me all this over breakfast while giving me directions.

'Come in.'

Thick curtains shut out the sun. A tired face softened by waves of white hair, a gentle smile. Marianna Nikolaevna sets aside some papers and gestures to a chair. 'Nadezhda Ivanovna tells me you want to talk about the siege.'

'If you don't mind.'

'Not at all. It is painful to remember those years of course.' She coughs. 'Excuse me, I have only just returned to work. I have been ill.'

My discomfort returns. I am asking this woman to relive past trauma. Yet my interest is not academic; there is a thread stretching between the siege and my own experience in Samara.

Marianna folds her hands on the desk. 'The hunger was the worst thing.' She closes her eyes. 'A man is walking across the Tyutchev Bridge, his figure is black against the snow. He moves slowly. It must be a public holiday because he is carrying some beer bottles – he has collected them on his ration cards. He is coming towards me – we are almost level when he stops. His eyes glaze over and he sinks to his knees.' She pauses.

A clock ticks through the silence.

'For a moment I imagine the man is about to pray. His torso sways and he topples forward into the snow, his bottles scatter around him. I walk over, bend down and touch his wrist. It is already cold.'

Marianna Nikolaevna's fingers twist together, their knuckles white.

'Bodies lay on the snow wherever they fell. Eventually they were dragged into piles but collection vans didn't come round very often so you had to pass these heaps of corpses whenever you went out.'

My eyes drift around the room. Its walls are lined with shelves, packed with cardboard files, repositories of the past. I picture Elizabeth, Empress of all the Russias, passing her days in this palace playing cards and telling fortunes, beneath the scornful eyes of her daughter-in-law, the future Catherine the Great.

Marianna's quiet voice goes on, 'I went out to look for children who had been pupils here. We found them in filthy apartments, traumatised, starving and cold. Some had frostbitten legs. Many had been abandoned because their parents had died or gone to the front.'

When Larisa was pulled from the ruins of her apartment block she was taken to a children's home – perhaps this one, she could not remember much about that time. All she could say was that she danced. I had thought she was confused, that it would not have been possible. But no, they had music, she insisted.

'The official opening of the Palace was in the spring of 1942,' Marianna continues. 'An army orchestra came to play. But the children could not dance; they could barely move at all. It was painful to watch them trying to stand, to move their limbs. They wobbled and collapsed to the floor.

'We fed them and gradually they regained their strength. They had lessons on the ground floor which was safer from shelling, but the rooms were cold and dark. Our home-made stoves didn't give out enough heat. The windows were boarded up as all their glass had been shattered. We were target 192 for German artillery fire.'

Involuntarily I glance up at the ceiling, as though expecting a shell to burst through its ornate tracery.

'We decided to organise the children into song and dance troupes. They performed at the front, on battleships too, and in hospitals. We feared for the wounded, that they might lose their will to live. Teachers who had worked in the Palace hospital at the beginning of the siege had seen this happen. But when they saw those children the patients would clap and cheer. Those with only one hand would slap their blankets. The children reminded them that their sacrifice had not been in vain.

'Our most famous troupe was the Obrant. One of its dancers was hit in the leg by a shell. She couldn't dance after that. Valentina Pavlovna Suleikina. You should talk to her. I'll give you her phone number.'

Marianna Nikolaevna slides a photograph towards me across her desk. Boys and girls, fierce in Cossack hat and baggy pants, leap through the air with drawn sabres.

'And you, Marianna Nikolaevna?'

Her face brightens. 'I was director of our children's choir. Now I am compiling a history of our department.'

She coughs again. 'Excuse me. Just after the siege we tried to forget – but of course that was impossible. Our experiences have made us what we are today. Look at me for example: I am seventy-seven and a second-category invalid. I have to care for my bedridden sister at home. Yet I still work.'

❦

Dostoevsky was once imprisoned in a cell on a corner of the Haymarket. He would have looked out onto a scene little different to that of today, a throng of street traders, drunks and petty criminals peddling knocked-off goods. In *Crime and Punishment* he writes: *The heat in the street was terrible: and the airlessness, the bustle and the plaster, scaffolding, bricks and dust all about him, and that special Petersburg stench, so familiar to all who are unable to get out of town in summer...*

Drunks, homeless children and stray dogs spill across tram tracks. In the middle of the square is a building site. Concrete slabs ring a pile of shacks and a rusting crane. Added to Dostoevsky's *insufferable stench from the pot-houses* is the miasma of rancid fat, pumped out by a McDonald's.

Rodion Raskolnikov knelt in Haymarket square to pray for forgiveness after he had murdered the old money-lender.

A ragged boy runs alongside the tram, brandishing a fifty rouble note, his face radiant.

'He doesn't know how much it's worth,' says a woman in the seat opposite.

'Only that it means sweets,' says her companion.

'Or glue,' says the first.

I alight from the tram and start to cross the square towards the metro. A policeman bars my way. He shakes his head and points in the direction I have come. Behind him an ambulance edges through the mass of traders and shoppers. I turn around and walk back as fast as I can to Nevsky where I pick up the metro from Gostinnii Dvor. I am due to have supper with Aunt Nadya and I don't want to keep her waiting.

The door swings open as I put my key in the lock.

'I'm so sorry...' I begin.

But Aunt Nadya shakes her head.

'There was an accident at the metro. They have just shown it on the news. The roof collapsed. Seven people were killed. We were worried about you.'

'What caused it?'

'They are blaming the builders. Substandard materials. They will hold an investigation into corruption.'

Aunt Nadya shrugs. 'Or so they say. Some of the locals take a different view. You know that building site?'

'In the middle of the square?'

'Where nothing is ever built. A church once stood there. It was demolished in 1961. The bulldozers came at night to avoid the protestors. I was among them. I don't go to church of course, but it is our heritage.' She walks over to switch off the television. 'Ever since, people have said there is a curse on the place.'

Divination was Larisa's other passion. Her only friend was the neighbourhood fortune-teller. Like the old Empress Elizabeth, she would sit for hours at the card table, picking over omens and portents of imminent catastrophe. She once warned me that the Nazis would return. With their allies the Russian fascists, they would stage a putsch in Moscow and seize power. Then everything would be different, we would see.

Aunt Nadya and I sit out on the balcony until late in the evening, watching the sky blaze mauve, orange and pink. Tonight the sun will not fall below the horizon for more than three hours.

'How is Marianna Nikolaevna?'

'Tired and not very well. Yet she goes to that office every day to compile the history of her department.'

'She has to. Don't you see? It keeps her going.'

'She spoke about how she rescued abandoned children from flats.'

Aunt Nadya's jaw tightens. 'Many of us were left alone, our parents dead or gone to the front.'

'And what about yours, Nadezhda Ivanovna?'

'Our mother was at the front. I was left alone with my younger sister, Lena's mother.'

A few miles outside the city, a front line of Soviet troops held off the invading Germans. Three hundred thousand died before the city was liberated.

'Was your father at the front too?'

A moment's hesitation. 'Our father... No. We lost him before the war. Anyway, my sister and I were starving. It was November 1941. We lay on our beds too weak to move. Marianna Nikolaevna picked up my sister and carried her downstairs to a sledge. Then she sent some passing soldiers in to help me down. I was so grateful to her for saving our lives but when I tried to thank her she brushed me aside. 'If I hadn't found you someone else would have,' was all she said.'

'She spoke about one of the Palace dancers who was wounded.'

'Call her.'

'Out of the blue like this? After all these years. Will she want to talk about it?'

'Why not?'

'Perhaps it will upset her to revive memories.'

'Perhaps it is your own reaction that worries you.'

She snatches the piece of paper from my hand, strides into the kitchen and picks up the phone.

'Hallo, hallo, Valentina Pavlovna? I have someone here who would like to talk to you. A foreigner, yes. A guest.'

She hands me the receiver. 'Talk to her. Go on. Don't worry. You will ask the right questions.'

***

Valentina Pavlovna's flat is in the old Kolomna area of the city, where dark canal waters mirror crumbling eighteenth-century mansions. I plunge into a labyrinth of courtyards. Scarcely penetrated by the sun, they stretch back from the road, one leading into another, ochre walls stained by damp and moss. The spectre of Raskolnikov slinks through their shadows.

A corner of one block is eroded with pockmarks – shell scars. Further down the street I pass a gap where a tenement has been torn down, iron cross-beams preventing the buildings on either side from toppling into the abyss. Images flood my mind of the empty lots that once pitted London, the silhouettes of fireplaces and vanished staircases, the exposed strips of faded wallpaper on blind walls.

A dank passage leads to Valentina's door. A woman with a pale and mournful face opens it. Limping heavily, she ushers me into her single room. 'Sit down, sit down. Look through this album of war photographs. I'll be with you in a minute. I'm just going to make coffee.'

A cry from the kitchen. Valentina leans against a wall, breathing heavily. I fetch her a glass of water.

'Thank you. A dizzy spell. It will pass. I suffer from low blood pressure. Please excuse me.'

'Perhaps I should leave you…'

'No, no, I'll be all right. It's just that I like to be on form when I meet people.'

I carry the tray of coffee and biscuits back to her room. We seat ourselves at her table.

'I believe you know the Anichkov Palace?'

'I spoke to Marianna Nikolaevna there.'

Valentina sighs. 'We lived a fairy-tale existence then, when it was the Palace of Pioneers. But life changed completely with the outbreak of war. At the time I was living with my elder brother and his family. My parents had…' She checks herself. 'I had lived with him since I was twelve. He left for the front. His wife and two children were evacuated to Siberia.'

'Did your parents die young?'

A pause. 'Yes.'

A wound still too raw to touch. If Valentina was sixteen in 1941 then her parents would have died in 1937. At that time Stalin's repression was at its height.

'We were talking about the siege...'

'Well, after my brother's family left I had no relatives in the city except Aunt Olya who lived upstairs. She had been a formidable woman but during that winter she grew weak and swollen from hunger. She suffered from diarrhoea and could no longer get out of bed. I would go to the Neva for water and drag the bucket back on my sledge to wash her. The task did not revolt me. She was actually the aunt of my brother's wife. All the same she would seize my hand and kiss it as I worked. "My own niece would not care for me better than you do."'

'One night I went to a neighbour's flat to warm myself. Leaving Aunt Olya with a wick lamp and covering the windows, I went upstairs. In the morning I came down to her room and called her name. There was no reply. I pushed open the door and pulled the blackout material from the window. Her lifeless body lay on the bed.' Valentina's voice shrinks to a whisper. 'Aunt Olya's arm hung down to the floor. Its flesh was gnawed away. White fat glistened beneath her skin.'

A biscuit is halfway to my mouth. I set it down on the plate.

'Rats?'

She nods. 'They were hungry too.'

The rungs of the chair dig into my spine. As I shift to find a more comfortable position my eyes catch a brilliant patch of blue beyond the window. I must go to the sea again today. I'll walk out of here and catch the hydrofoil from the Tyutchev pier to Kronstadt. The wind and salt spray will revive me. I touch my tongue to my lips.

The chink of a cup against a saucer brings me back to the room.

'You used to see the rats running in packs through the city, crazed, searching for food. When I slept on our stove I would take up the heaviest things I could find – books and shoes – and throw them down when they became too noisy. In the end they all died too – sometimes people ate them.'

She pushes a plate of biscuits towards me. 'Take some more.'

'Oh, no thank you.' I force a smile.

I wonder what horror Larisa carried with her on the lorry across the ice. One day she flew into a rage with Ivan because he had not bought her the large-screen TV set that she wanted. 'Do we live in the stone age?' she screamed at him. The next minute she heard a bird chirruping in the tree-top outside her window. Drying her tears, she took my hand and led me out onto the balcony to listen.

It was as though a part of her had been left behind in the rubble of her bombed-out Leningrad home.

'What did you do then?' I ask Valentina. 'You were on your own.'

'I decided to go to the front,' she replies. 'Rations were better there. I trained as a telephonist at an artillery post and became very quick at the work.

'Then I heard a radio announcement that the ballet master Arkadii Obrant had formed a dance troupe of children from the Palace of Pioneers. I went to him and asked if I could join. By then I had been through so much that I never imagined that I would dance again. I even doubted that I could. But watching the others gave me confidence and I soon completed my training.'

She bites her lower lip.

'But my career was brought to an end by a shell. It

exploded when I was on my way to give a performance near the front. I never danced again.'

Valentina hands me a photograph of herself as a young woman. The same mournful eyes and drooping cheeks.

'Keep it.'

I drop the photo into my bag.

'I would like you to have these too.' Valentina Pavlovna presses some folded pages into my hand. 'When I heard you were coming I sat up till three in the morning writing down my story.'

'Thank you.'

'You see,' a faint rose suffuses her cheeks, 'books and films based on my character have been made in this country.' She glances at me shyly. 'I would like to think that one day something about me might appear in English.'

❧

We danced in forests, near the front line. Gunfire and explosions ceased to bother us – we no longer took cover. At times we had to disguise our bright costumes from the attention of enemy planes. At other times, when the enemy were close, we danced without music. Straw was laid beneath our feet to muffle our stamping. We danced Ukrainian gopak, Armenian, Belorussian, Red Army, Red Navy dances.

It is morning and I am sitting in the Summer Garden by the Fontanka reading Valentina Pavlovna's story.

One fresh sunny day I set off to give a concert. I skipped along a railway line from sleeper to sleeper. A sudden force knocked me off my feet. I fell, hitting my head. With a great effort I raised my head. My foot was twisted at an angle. A fountain of blood spurted from my leg.

A couple wander past my bench, arm-in-arm. The woman makes a remark and the man bursts into laughter. Beyond them a party of German tourists clusters around a monument to the fabulist Krylov.

They loaded me into a lorry and took me to hospital. I lay in shock while the doctors fought to save my life. As long as I retained consciousness I kept wondering how I was going to dance again.

I lay in bed for a year. The doctors saved my leg but my youth and beauty were shattered. I lost my profession. Everything I had studied since the age of seven was gone.

Now, on the eve of my seventy-fifth birthday, I still need massage and other treatments. Wounds remain with us forever. You can treat them but they continue to live by their own malign laws. They manifest themselves in pain, ill-health, and above all, in memory.

I lower the papers onto my lap and stare into the overgrown beds of the Summer Garden. A blackbird hops among dandelion clocks and wilting lilies-of-the-valley. The couple on the next bench wrap their arms around each other. In some other, parallel existence, they kiss.

8

Knock on my door with your little fist – I'll open it.
I always opened it for you.
Now I am beyond the high mountains,
Beyond the desert, beyond the wind and the heat,
But I shall never abandon you…
I did not hear you moan
You did not ask me for bread.
Bring me a maple twig
Or simply a bunch of grass,
As you brought last spring.
And bring a palmful of cold, pure Neva water
I'll wash the traces of blood
From your little golden head…
Anna Akhmatova – written in memory of Valya
Smirnov, a neighbour boy killed by a bomb during
the siege.

Tiny claws catch in my hair. A prehensile tail drags across my cheek. I try to move but my head is weighted to the pillow. It is one of those terrifying awakenings when the physical body still sleeps. I fight my way into the daylight world, tearing my head from the pillow, my heart pounding. A rustle in the corner. A sharp squeak. Silence.

With shaking hands I reach for the heavy dictionary on the bedside table. Armed now, I stuff my feet into slippers and creep over to the wall. No holes in the wainscoting, nowhere for a rat to hide. My stomach heaves. In the kitchen I pour a glass of water. Lena is already up, swallowing a cup of tea before work.

'What happened?'

Water splashes on the floor.

'Steady.'

'There was a rat. It crawled over my head.'

Lena sets down her cup. 'There are no rats up here. Nor mice even. Cockroaches sometimes. This is the seventh floor. The building is concrete, no cracks or holes. Come with me. Look.'

We inspect the walls and flooring. She is right. Part of me doesn't want to believe it. The alternative is worse.

'You see?'

'I felt it on my face.'

Lena's voice is firm. 'But what did you see?'

'I heard a squeak.'

Lena squeezes my shoulder. 'I have to give a couple of lessons after work but I shall be free by nine. Meet me at a quarter past outside the Philarmonia.'

She leaves.

The nausea lingers. I pace the flat, attempting to tidy up, but my eyes drift to corners of the room.

I need to go to the railway office today to book my return ticket well in advance.

A plate slips from my hands and shatters.

I walk into the bedroom, pull out my case, extract my passport and a wad of cash.

I take Boldyrev with me for company. It will be a long wait in the railway office.

Outside, the streets are busy. The pedestrian subway is packed with bemedalled pensioners selling Communist literature, youths in black leather peddling heavy metal tapes, men and women with basketsful of kittens. At the far end of the passage an old lady with swollen legs plays the violin. I listen for a minute, drop a few roubles into her case and walk on. The tram arrives. A woman on the opposite seat reads a book entitled *The Writer and Suicide*. Sweat trickles down my sides; my temples throb. There is a sour metallic taste in my mouth, like blood. Alighting at the stop past the Anichkov bridge on Nevsky I walk down Liteiny Prospect. Ahead of me a tall white building shimmers in the heat haze. 'The Big House' is Petersburg's equivalent of Moscow's Lubianka, home of the secret police. Perhaps a quarter of the city's adult population passed through its doors during the terror of the 1930s.

A self-service snack bar stands on a corner, all pink plastic and plate glass. But it promises air conditioning and by now my head is spinning. I need to fortify myself before the railway office. I have a sudden flashback to Samara, of standing in line for two hours only to be sent to another queue. The second cashier slammed down a closed for lunch sign just as I reached her.

Buying water and salad from the counter, I take my tray over to an empty table by the window and sit down with a pang of guilt for having spent the equivalent of Lena's weekly teacher's wage.

Opening Boldyrev, I read a cryptic entry: *Somewhere around the 26th and 28th December 1941 I finished an incredibly stupid story… 'Two Travels to the Big House'.* He writes this title in English, as a precaution. Even under siege conditions he never knew when his flat might be searched, his papers seized.

As Boldyrev and countless others discovered, the terror did not end with the outbreak of war. The NKVD were as scared of their own citizens as they were of the invaders, perhaps more so. They feared a reaction to siege conditions – the bread riots that triggered the overthrow of the Tsar in 1917 were only a generation away. Never mind that the situation in 1941 was far worse and that people in the final stages of starvation do not make revolutions.

The smoked glass of the café window bestows a patina of age upon the Big House, so that it resembles a building in an old film. Boldyrev once walked up those front steps, summoned to participate in his incredibly stupid story.

❧

A policeman sits in a warm, well-lit office, looking down on Liteiny Prospect. Below him shawl-wrapped wraiths drag sledges through the snow. On the sledges are long bundles bound in sheets or curtains. A hand shakes loose from its shroud, skeletal, black and rigid, its fingers claw the air as though trying to extract nourishment. The scene is weirdly peaceful; no sounds rise from the street but the crunch of felt boots and the squeak of sledge runners on the snow. A tram is marooned in the middle of Liteiny, encased in a snow drift. Figures pass by in slow motion – one staggers and falls. Another stops and bends over him. He puts his arms around the fallen man, apparently in a gesture of assistance. But the policeman sees a furtive pat down, a search for bread, money or a ration card. He makes a mental note.

In the bowels of the building a canteen serves meat

and noodles, tea and vodka. Like the government, the police have their own dining-rooms and power supply; they inhabit islands of warmth and light that float above the city's frozen darkness. But still the policeman is afraid. He is afraid of losing his ticket to the dining-room, of losing his lamp light and radiator. He fears losing his power of life and death over his fellow citizens. What he fears most is his own vulnerability, although this fear is locked beneath his conscious mind.

The fear makes him insane. He hounds his fellow citizens, hauling them in for interrogation and torture. A leaflet was found on Vasilievsky Island, calling for a hunger demonstration. This leaflet unnerves the policeman more than German bombs; he despatches hundreds of operatives to track down its author. He arrests a woman in a bread queue. According to his informant she was complaining of hunger; he hears counter-revolutionary defeatism. He arrests a doctor for releasing death rate figures; a work of anti-Soviet agitation. He pronounces the death sentence on the already dead, on those who have cut the flesh from corpses and eaten it. He does battle with subversion everywhere; projecting a demonic shadow play over the city.

The policeman was orphaned after the revolution, during the civil war. In 1918 he found himself on the streets. He was ten years old. He lived in the Vitebsk station, sleeping with other homeless children by the hot water pipes in a basement beneath the left luggage department. He begged from passengers and stole what he could. The secret police rounded him up and sent him to an orphanage. Later they recruited him; he had no other loyalties.

After the siege was lifted the policeman fell victim to his own terror and was shot on the orders of a friend and close colleague. For it happened that when there was almost no one left to feed upon, the agents of terror turned upon each other, just as in the final stages of starvation the body feeds upon itself.

I drain my glass and put Boldyrev back into my bag. For reasons that we shall never learn he was released from the Big House in December 1941, back into the starving city.

※

I take a shortcut through an alleyway between high yellow walls. It leads into a garden laid out behind the eighteenth-century Sheremetev Palace. Pathways straggle among maples and tall limes. The garden is neglected, its fountains have dried up and yet it feels like a refuge from the heat and chaos of the city. I sit down on a bench already occupied by an elderly woman. Despite the heat she wears a stained grey coat, open at the front to expose vest straps hanging from fragile clavicles. Her toes curl through fraying sandals. A string bag of newspaper-wrapped packages lies between us on the bench. Something about the bag strikes a familiar and disturbing chord, but I can't make the connection.

The woman acknowledges me with a nod. 'They are turning off the water again tomorrow.'

'It is the same with us.' A notice on the wall of Lena's entranceway announces that there will be no hot water for a month, 'for technical reasons'.

Now an image comes to me, a photo of the siege, a street scene. Those same string bags dangling from the arms of walking corpses, weighted at the bottom by one newspaper-wrapped package, one precious ration.

'I can't sit in my room.' The woman leans towards me confidentially. 'It is too hot. I don't sleep at night. Is it hot where you are?'

'Very hot.'

'I don't remember a hotter summer than this.'

She points up to a window in a rear wing of the palace. 'Did you know that Anna Akhmatova once had rooms here?'

'No, I didn't.'

'This was the 'House on the Fontanka' of her poems. They've turned it into a museum now. It's closed today. For technical reasons.'

I study my companion more closely. Despite the shabbiness of her clothes, her patrician nose, hooded eyes and beautifully arranged white hair echo Akhmatova herself.

A plump woman with a white stick taps her way along the path. She stops before our bench.

'Would you like to sit?'

'Yes.'

I grasp her clammy wrist and guide her onto the bench.

'You are not from around here?'

'From England.'

'Ah…' A pause. 'Queen Elizabeth.'

'And what are you doing in Petersburg?' asks the dignified woman.

I hesitate for a moment. They are old enough. 'I am talking to people about the siege.'

I remind myself that I am on my way to the railway office. There was no need to bring up the siege again.

'Oh, the siege,' says the blind woman. 'It was terrible. I ate nothing for two months.' Her voice rises to a wail. 'They said, "She'll die today, she'll die today for sure."'

'But you survived.'

The woman smiles with satisfaction. 'The doctor gave

me some pills. I don't know what they were but they saved me. All my hair fell out but I survived.'

The dignified woman is staring straight ahead, ignoring our conversation. 'Have you been to the Park of Rest and Culture?'

She brushes my arm. A rotted leather watchstrap binds the bones and veins of her wrist as though they were a bundle of twigs.

'No.'

'It's very beautiful. You need to take the Number 12 tram…'

'No, no, it's much easier to go by metro to Chornaya Rechka, and then take the Number 27 bus,' the blind woman interrupts.

'But they stopped that one ages ago.'

'No, they didn't, I don't know where you get your information from…'

They fall silent. The tall maple beside Akhmatova's window rustles. A heat-shrivelled leaf drops to the ground.

'Of course we lived much better in Stalin's time,' the dignified woman remarks. 'Now our country is full of bandits…'

'Thieves and bandits,' the blind woman echoes. I feel glad Aunt Nadya is not here to argue with them. Yet these ladies voice a lament I have heard before, over the years, here and in Moscow and by the Volga. A strange choice of golden age. As though Stalin's terror could have left these women untouched, allowing them to file him away in a memory drawer marked 'cheap sausage and safe streets'.

But perhaps the past is the only place where they find solace. Was I not searching for something similar when I arrived, walking around Lena's neighbourhood, scouring dusty streets for a part of my life that will never return?

'Do your parents remember the war?' asks the dignified lady.

'My father was an officer, a gunner, defending the
Arctic convoys.'

'Thank him,' they say in unison.

He is ill now, crippled with Parkinson's. But he
remains a Russophile, full of admiration for their culture
and the way they fought the war. Swallowing a lump in
my throat, I rise from the bench. It is time to meet Lena.

'Goodbye ladies. It was very pleasant talking to you.'

'Goodbye, goodbye.'

❦

She is waiting on Nevsky outside the Philarmonia.

A cool hand slips into the crook of my arm. 'How are
you now?'

'Better, thanks. It must have been a nightmare. But
it shook me.'

The hand tightens on my arm.

'I meant to book my ticket home in advance but
somehow I never reached the railway offices. I sat for
too long behind the Sheremetev Palace.'

'Beguiled, like Gerda in the flower garden?'

'You read the *Snow Queen* too?'

She nods. 'Come on.'

She leads me through Palace Square behind the
Hermitage to a road lined with mansions. 'Millionaire's
Row. Nabokov was born in that house on the corner, the
one with the huge bay window.'

We walk on across the Field of Mars where one last
white peony clings to a bush. I bend to catch its scent.
A woman with straggling blonde hair weaves down the

path towards us. 'Look!' Her vodka breath envelops us as she points to the sky.

A single cloud of deep fuchsia tinged with gold drifts through a violet mist. The drunk stops everyone she meets until the Field of Mars is dotted with watchers of the sky.

'And this is the city where people talk to themselves more often than to each other,' says Lena.

We walk along the Embankment, past a row of black Mercedes saloons parked outside a nightclub. Shadows flicker behind curtains. *Ra, ra, Rasputin, lover of the Russian Queen* reverberates along the empty street.

It is almost midnight and the sky is electric pink.

'Those poor people.' Lena nods towards the flickering windows. 'To be missing this.'

Ivan loved the natural world and hated parties, restaurants and nightclubs. Yet night after night he would haunt Samara's clubs and bars, sidling up to their habitués, making deals, effortlessly charming, endlessly calculating.

Unlike his mother, however, he was not acquisitive. He made no personal fetish of consumer goods. He drove a modest Zhiguli. A Mercedes would advertise his wealth, attract unwelcome attention. He did not want things, he said; he wanted people.

Lena and I cross the Troitsky bridge, stopping to gaze back at the windows of the Hermitage blazing gold.

A statue of the poet stands inside Pushkin metro. Flowers lie at his feet.

9

In our six-room apartment
There live only three of us – you and I
And the wind blowing from the darkness…
No, excuse me. I am mistaken.
There is a fourth lying out on the balcony,
Waiting a week for the funeral.
Zinaida Shishova

'Are you ready for another?' Aunt Nadya asks me over dinner.

'Another what?'

'*Blokadnik.*' She hands me a slice of rye bread. 'I've made an appointment for you this morning. At eleven. You are to be on the bridge of sphinxes. You know the one I mean, on the Fontanka.'

I set off through streets swept by a fresh morning breeze, my voice recorder in my bag, with the precious blank cassettes that I scoured the city to find.

As I approach the little bridge guarded by stone sphinxes, a slim woman in a yellow beret steps forward to greet me. 'I am Irina. I will take you to meet my mother.

She says she wants to tell you the truth about the siege.'

I follow Irina along the canal and through an arch-way into a dusty courtyard. A stray dog lifts its head and then sinks back into apathy. A fly crawls over an encrusted eye. Stepping over fragments of bone, Irina turns her key in a metal outer door.

The front door is opened by an upright elderly lady dressed neatly in black; her grey hair scraped back and fastened by tortoiseshell combs like those my grand-mother used to wear. 'I am Galina Popova.'

They usher me into a room almost entirely taken up by a long oak table laden with salads and dumplings. 'Come in, come in.' Galina indicates a straight-backed chair. 'Do sit down. These are all my worldly belong-ings.' Her arm sweeps around the room. 'I have no car, no dacha, but I live very well. I am a war veteran, so I travel free on public transport and my pension is good.'

Her face darkens. 'Mind you, I know people who left the city in the first week of war and today you see them sporting medals. You can buy everything in the Haymarket. Passports – whatever you like. While the authorities sleep.'

She picks up a pair of silver tongs. 'I am a true *blokadnitsa*. I remained in Leningrad throughout the siege. I saw my father die of hunger. Have some *piroshki*. Mushroom and cabbage.'

She drops some fluffy dumplings onto my plate. 'You know, there were people who enriched themselves during the siege. They filled their apartments with antiques and rugs. Our family sold everything for food but at least we lived with clear consciences. We did not profit from the misfortune of others.'

I put down my fork, beset by an image of Ivan. Dressed in a long leather coat and fur hat, he is standing in the Haymarket, examining a gold necklace as though it were a fake. I can see quite well how he would have survived, had he lived through the siege.

I wonder what I would have done myself.

'Under those circumstances people must have changed…'

'Oh, they changed alright – beyond all recognition. Would you like some cranberry juice? It is home-made.' Irina pours the ruby liquid from an old-fashioned glass jug etched with flowers.

'Let me tell you about the time a school friend came to visit. She brought her mother with her, who was a famous singer with the Kirov. We made an effort to welcome them. "Ladies, we have two spoonfuls of porridge," my mother said, "we shall divide them into four." We sat down to eat. The singer sat perched like a hawk, her eyes never leaving her daughter's plate. I'll never forget her expression, never.'

Galina pushes aside the dumplings on her plate. A tear slides down her cheek. 'As we neared the end of the meal,' she whispers, 'the singer suddenly reached out and scooped up a portion of her daughter's porridge. Oh yes, starvation is the worst thing of all.'

I stare down at the tablecloth. 'Excuse me.'

'No,' says Galina, wiping her eyes. 'We have to talk about our experiences – we have to learn from them. Otherwise what did we suffer for? Without a doubt, hunger deprives people of their reason. When a person is starving the brain starts to die.'

She hands me tea in a delicate cup of Lomonosov china. 'I don't think a human being can see worse sights than those I witnessed as a seventeen-year-old. We could not escape. There was nowhere to run from the bombing, the cold and the hunger.

'When war broke out my parents refused to leave the city. My father said we had to stay to defend Leningrad.

My sister went to the front. We wanted to be here so she could return to us when she had leave.'

Galina lowers her voice. 'She is very old now. Come and say hello to her.'

She takes me out to the kitchen. A white-haired woman in a faded housecoat bends over a saucepan, slowly stirring its contents.

'This is our guest from England,' Galina shouts.

Her sister raises her head and nods but her eyes are turned somewhere deep within herself.

'People began to die,' says Galina when we return to the living-room. 'One day in winter I was hurrying home through the snow when a goods lorry drove past me. Its back doors were not properly shut and corpses were spilling out onto the road. They lay scattered: women in headscarves, children, some naked... They were already rigid. The driver was too far ahead for me to shout at him. I ran home and burst into tears. 'We could be those corpses,' said my mother. And she was right. There was only the thinnest line between the living and the dead.'

I spoon beetroot salad onto my plate and help myself to more *piroshki*.

'We lived by a school that was full of refugees from villages around Leningrad. They slept packed together on blankets on the floor. I heard rumours of murder among the refugees – I don't know the exact details.'

She takes a sip of juice. 'All I know is what I saw with my own eyes. One day...' Her voice quivers. 'One day when I was crossing the school yard I came upon the body of a woman with the flesh of her buttocks cut away.'

I lay down my fork, aware that I have been shovelling food into my mouth without tasting it.

'Weren't you scared to walk by yourself?'

'My father would come out and meet me on my way home from work. Although I was a slender girl, emaciated by hunger, I looked rather plump when I went outdoors because I wore two coats, one on top of the other.'

❧

The meal has been cleared away. The afternoon draws on. I sit on the sofa with a heavy velvet-covered album on my lap. Close, copperplate handwriting, Edwardian bosoms and picture hats, babies in christening gowns, phantom smiles fading into white. The years fall through my fingers. Flat World War One caps are replaced by pointed Tukhachevsky hats with stars on the front. Girls in tractor-print dresses throw back their heads and laugh, arms around each other's shoulders. On the last page, a young man in a flying jacket.

'In 1943 I fell in love for the first time. His name was Alexander. He was a pilot. 30 March was my birthday. Alexander had leave and bought tickets for *Bayardère*. I felt so proud and happy sitting beside my beloved in the Musical Comedy, well you can imagine… I had even removed my headscarf. I had rather nice hair in those days.' Galina pats her grey bun and smiles to herself. 'During the aria I closed my eyes and floated off to a far-away place where I sat with Alexander in a satin dress, well-fed and happy. In the interval he reached into the pocket of his leather pilot's jacket and produced a slab of American chocolate. I had not tasted chocolate in a long time. "What should I do with that?" I asked. He laughed. Alexander was killed in his plane in 1944.'

Tears spring to my eyes. How did you bear it, I want to ask. You were so young.

Galina picks up a framed photograph from the dresser. A smiling baby in a red knitted cap reaches out his arms. 'My first great-grandchild. He was born this winter. I have kept my siege diary for him so that when he grows up he will know what our family went through.

'I am so proud that he is named Alexander.'

10

Clouds stood on end, like hair,
over the pale, smoking Neva
Boris Pasternak

The bell chirrups and a striking man of indeterminate age stands before us. His hair is still black but his face is ridged like an ancient mountain range. He must be from Central Asia, Uzbek at a guess.

He kisses Lena's hand. 'This is Osman,' she says. 'He is a poet.'

Osman does not smile but his dark eyes are warm.

'A great pleasure.' He kisses my hand in turn.

It is evening and Lena has insisted that I accompany her to 'a celebration'. We follow Osman down a bare corridor lit by one unshaded bulb. Chests piled with yellowing newspapers line the walls. In an unlit kitchen spectral limbs dangle from lines above antique stoves. Tripping over a child's sledge I step into a dish of cat food. A wave of nostalgia hits me for the communal flat where I lived in Samara.

That winter I felt as though I was buried beneath

a snowdrift on the far edge of Europe. Cosy evenings were spent drinking glasses of tea with my neighbours, women who had lived lives of hard work with little material reward, while snow muffled the outside world and frost coral branched over the window panes.

How selective the memory is, skipping over the gossip, the kitchen squabbles, the Friday night drunkenness and the morning queues for the toilet.

The flat was a relic of the 1917 revolution, when the houses of the wealthy were requisitioned and divided. Each room housed a couple or family. Stoves and sinks were crammed into the kitchen, there were two shared toilets and a trough for washing. We bathed at the neighbourhood bathhouse. For decades after the revolution most urban Soviet citizens lived in these *komunalki*, as they were called. Now the flats are being bought up and remodelled as private residences, their poorer inhabitants dispersed and moved on to who knows where.

Ivan hated the place. He said it was squalid. My impoverished elderly neighbours adored him.

Osman opens a door off the corridor. 'Lenochka darling!' A stout woman clad in a half-slip and an armour-plated bra flings her arms around Lena's neck. After being kissed repeatedly on both cheeks Lena extricates herself and introduces us. 'Naima Suleimanovna.'

'Delighted.' Gold teeth glint in the lamplight.

I take her for Osman's wife but she turns out to be his mother and they share this room. A flowered curtain hangs from a string stretched between two single beds.

'Are you married? No? Well never mind, you're a pretty girl. We'll find you a nice Russian husband. Would you like that?' Naima's chin wobbles as she laughs, which she does all the time. She pulls a shiny pink blouse over her head.

'Pouff, it must have shrunk in the wash. Lenochka,

you are too thin, can you pull up this zip?' She tucks rolls of flesh beneath the waistband of her slip and pats them down.

Lena obliges.

Naima worked in a rubber factory all her life and has just retired, she tells me, as she fastens her earrings and adjusts her neckline in a spotted mirror.

'Okay girls, let's go!' She pats her oiled coiffure, sprays scent into her cleavage, squeezes her feet into a pair of pink stilettos and sashays ahead of us into the next room. 'We've arrived!' She holds out her arms as though we'd just got off the Trans-Siberian express and not emerged from behind the dividing wall.

Naima's neighbours are seated around the table, a familiar cast: an overexcited middle-aged man; his resigned wife; a beautiful woman with tragic eyes; some younger people and a cluster of *babushki* at the far end. A couple sit at the head of the table, the young man awkward in his overlarge suit. They appear to be still in their teens. Their baby sleeps behind them in a basket. He has just been christened; Lena is godmother.

'At last!' The excited man seizes a bottle and glides around the table, bowing to the ladies as he fills their glasses. I guess he is the baby's grandfather. I am seated between Osman and the tragic woman. She sighs. I open my mouth to introduce myself but close it again. She is intent upon the progress of the bottle.

Its neck protrudes from a hairy hand beside my shoulder. 'Ladies.'

My neighbour doesn't move a muscle.

The host is back at his seat, glass raised.

'Ladies and gentlemen, a toast to Vadim Dmitrich.'

'Vadim Dmitrich!'

The baby sleeps on.

Icy fingers close around my palm and raise it to

the light. The table falls silent. 'You have had some unpleasantness in your life, a blow has befallen you,' she says. 'But don't despair; you have two very strong guardian angels.'

'Let's drink to the angels,' the host slurs.

'How is that possible?' Naima glares across the table. 'We only have one each.'

The tragic woman fixes her with a look of contempt. 'Naima Suleimanovna, you read cards and I read hands. Let us not trespass upon one another.'

Naima struggles to her feet. Hoisting her bosom, she turns to face our host. 'Let's fill our glasses and drink a toast – to men!'

I lift my glass and set it down again untouched, with Ivan's voice in my ears. He never drank vodka. As a young boy he had seen what it did to people. His father had been an alcoholic who deserted the family when he was a baby.

One night after a party like this on the Volga we wandered home across a sparkling snowfield, entranced by the beauty of the night. I ended up in a military hospital. My kidneys recovered but after that I heeded Ivan's warning.

Something like a cold wind brushes my bare arm.

'What's that, lemonade?' she whispers, her breath sour.

The others have drained their glasses in one, Russian style.

I look into the woman's eyes and see Boldyrev's Uncle Sasha.

I don't think this will help you, I want to say. But she already knows. I bite my lip and slide my glass over to her plate. If she drinks quickly enough – and she will – she can pretend she is still toasting the child. Otherwise she will have to wait for another bottle to be opened and another toast to be proposed. Like almost everything else, Russian drinking is a communal affair with its own codes of conduct.

'It's despair,' whispers Osman into my left ear.

'I know.'

He reaches under the table and squeezes my hand.

❦

The host snores in a corner beside the child; the *babushki* have gone to bed. Drunk beyond words, Naima and the young people have taken to the floor where they stamp and shake to a manic pop tune. The tragic woman left when the vodka ran out.

We slip unnoticed from the wreckage of the table and let ourselves out of the flat. Osman escorts us home. On the embankment a crowd has gathered by the Troitsky bridge. Tonight in celebration of midsummer there will be a simultaneous raising of all the Neva's road bridges. We stop to watch a nacreous streak push through asphalt and iron.

'Hurrah!' cries the crowd as the streak widens.

Bridges all along the river split and raise their arms in salute to the sleepless sky. Vessels of all sorts, launches, pleasure cruisers and a bulk cargo ship, come to a halt and sound their whistles.

'Hurrah!' the crowd roars again.

'Let's go,' says Lena.

Osman walks between us, his arms linked through ours. 'Where did you learn Russian?' he asks me.

'In a *komunalka* by the Volga.'

'But you are English?'

'Yes.'

'No Russian ancestry?' His eyes narrow.

'None at all.'

He shakes his head. 'Extraordinary. You speak as though it was once your language and you were retrieving fragments of it – like the lines of a lost poem. I have never heard a foreigner speak the way you do.'

He comes up with us to the flat. We sit in Lena's kitchen drinking tea.

'Caroline has been talking to *blokadniki*.'

Her tone is almost resentful. I can't read her mood tonight. She may have drunk a lot.

Osman regards me thoughtfully. He has drunk nothing at all. I tell them about my visit to Galina and the story of the actress who ate her daughter's porridge.

Osman frowns. 'The other day I read about an actor who lost eleven members of his family. Only he and his wife were left. For the remaining nineteen years of her life his wife behaved as though the war had never taken place. At mealtimes she laid places on the table for all her dead relatives – children, brothers, sisters and aunts. At the sound of the doorbell she would call out to her son to answer it.'

'And perhaps they are still with us.' Lena gets up from her seat and starts to pace the kitchen. She picks up a painted wooden spoon and traces its pattern with a finger. Then she flings it into the sink. Turning, she catches sight of my voice recorder on the table. She pulls it towards her and presses the play button.

'We built bonfires in the hospital courtyard and threw in the soldiers' clothes as we undressed them.' Galina's voice fills the kitchen.

'I have never forgotten the noise lice make when they burn: tchok! tchok! tchok! Like small-arms fire. That fearful sound has remained with me all my life.

'We eventually got those men into beds in the wards and corridors. When I went home that night I cried. I felt helpless in the face of so much suffering.' Lena is listening intently now, head in her hands, eyes closed.

'I asked my mother what to do,' Galina's voice continues. 'She said, "Care for those boys, stroke their hands, whisper words of comfort. You will do all you can to help them."

'Many soldiers passed through our wards. But one of them has remained in my mind to this day. Kolya Lizhenko was twenty years old and had had both legs amputated. The surgeon told me they were going to amputate his right arm. Kolya cried all the time and we were ordered to keep watch on him. He refused to take food. He was fed intravenously while the doctors tried to convince him that life was worth living.

'Kolya's eyes would follow me around the ward with their question, "Why live? Give me one good reason."'

'For love,' says Osman.

'Ssh!' Lena frowns.

'Our political instructor told me to try to help him. It was hard. At seventeen what did I know of life? In his place I couldn't imagine wanting to carry on either. But I would stop by Kolya's bed, take his hand and tell him that he would grow stronger, he would meet people who would help him. He said he was alone, his parents must have died in Nazi-occupied Ukraine. "But why kill yourself?" I asked. "You will get prostheses." I told him about a pilot who had flown after his legs were amputated.'

Lena has risen from her stool and is pacing up and down the kitchen. Osman puts out a hand to hers but she brushes it away.

'Shall I stop the tape?'

'No, no, go on.'

'When I had the time I would sit with him. At first I would read Lermontov or Pushkin but after a while I realised that words were unnecessary. Then we would sit together in silence.'

My voice now. 'What happened to Kolya?'

'In the end he was evacuated. The hospital needed his bed. He was sent away across Lake Ladoga to convalesce. He wrote, *Children come to see me. I have made friends. A girl comes to shave me. She brings eau de Cologne.* We corresponded for a long time but lost touch in the end when we moved house.'

'So Kolya saved her,' says Osman.

'Galina?'

'Yes. As long as she cared for him – and the others – she would not succumb.'

Unlike that poor actress who stole food from her daughter's plate.

11

*Sometimes as dessert they distributed half tablets of
joiner's glue, while a piece of sturgeon isinglass (fish glue)
from the restoration stores proved the height of luxury.*
Boris Piotrovsky – former director of the Hermitage

'You need to stress the horror.' Mikhail Borisovich
Piotrovsky, director of the Hermitage, speaks excellent English.

I can hardly escape that, I think.

Target number nine for the Germans, the Hermitage
lay fourteen kilometres from the front line. I have seen
the pictures of bomb-damaged statues and ceilings, of
shattered windows, of snowdrifts in the halls. I know
that the corpses of museum staff who died were laid out
in the Small Hermitage, awaiting burial in spring. The
artists who lived in the basement shelters showed it all.

'Our resources are at your disposal.'

The Hermitage education department is a large high-ceilinged room, its tall windows looking out across the Neva to the Peter-Paul fortress. Landscapes in the bold brushstrokes of children cover the walls. Sunlight streams through the windows. A white pleasure boat sails past, chased by a flock of gulls.

Here in this room, on the afternoon of 10 December 1941, after the canteen had refused to serve him lunch, Alexander Boldyrev delivered a paper on the Central Asian poet Alisher Navoi. *Too many positive comments on my paper,* he wrote. *As dusk fell Mamma and I walked home through a hard frost amid the astonishing beauty of besieged Petersburg...*

Svetlana Moldovanovna welcomes me with tea. 'Do you write for children or adults?' she asks as she fills my cup.

Her question startles me. 'Adults. I don't know much about children.'

'Twelve- or thirteen-year-olds for example?'

'Oh, I see. I hope I write as clearly as that.'

❦

I stand before Rembrandt's *Old Man in Red*, barely aware of the processions of tourists trailing through the hall after the raised lollipops of their guides. The old man sits in deep contemplation, only his hands and face are illuminated. He has the inward gaze of Galina Popova's sister, of someone who already looks beyond this life.

The old man is not a *blokadnik*. After war broke out he was shipped to the Ural mountains.

'Two trains were sent to Sverdlovsk in July 1941. They

carried over a million paintings and statues.' Ludmila Voronikhina receives me in her office. 'After the evacuation guides took soldiers around the galleries, their words filling the empty frames as they described the paintings that once hung there.'

Ludmila is framed by a French door which gives onto a garden laid out around statues, fountains and a dovecote. Vegetable plots were dug here in the spring of '42, to feed the surviving members of staff.

'Our galleries were saved by a group of elderly women, former museum attendants. Imagine – most were in their seventies, some invalids, all of them starving. They worked ceaselessly, clearing snow from the halls. When it thawed they mopped up the melt water. One would fall ill and go to the hospital in the basement; another would take her place...

'My husband was head of security. He lived in the basement shelters with two thousand other museum workers. They gave lectures, wrote papers. When not on fire watch duty they spent their time sharing all they knew with each other, the older with the younger, so that their expertise would not die with them. It helped them bear their hunger.'

Never in my life, whether before the siege or after it, have I had such a definite, clearly defined aim in life... People acquired an amazing integrity... I felt as though something within me had been unleashed, set free... And [under shelling] *I would think what a fool I had been, living the way I used to live!* So wrote Pavel Gubchevsky, a researcher at the Hermitage.

They could not afford to let their creative powers stagnate. Then it was a matter of life and death; these days it is too easy to coast. I have been sleepwalking.

Svetlana appears and takes me down to a basement

gallery inhabited by classical gods and mythical beasts. 'Athene, Aphrodite, Eros – they are all *blokadniki*. They could not be evacuated from the museum in time. They were packed up and ready to go but the Germans closed their circle.'

We pass into the Hall of Jupiter. In the first-century AD his huge marble and bronze figure sat in the Roman villa of the Emperor Domitian; in the twentieth-century he sat here, throughout the bombardment of Leningrad, the winged goddess of victory in his right hand. Unlike Rembrandt's *Old Man* he was too large to be moved. Jupiter's left heel rests on its plinth, its instep and toes protrude. 'Blind children love this foot,' says Svetlana. 'We bring them down to this gallery to view the sculptures with their hands. They learn what a giant is. That panther too.' She indicates a crouching beast on a low pedestal in the centre of the gallery. 'They absorb classical beauty through their fingertips. We relate ancient myths to them and these take shape in their hands.'

❧

I leave the Hermitage and walk up Nevsky Prospect, the city's main thoroughfare. It runs across a loop of the Neva, from the Alexander Nevsky monastery on one bank to Admiralty Square on the other. Behind me Peter the Great rears on his stallion, the great Bronze Horseman of Pushkin's poem. Nevsky is lined with late-nineteenth-century apartment blocks, newly painted in ice cream colours: strawberry, caramel and pistachio. Traffic surges past prosperous shops and cafés, the art nouveau splendour of Yeliseev's grocery, the House of

Books. Today the scene seems ephemeral, a Potemkin village masking rubble and corpses.

As I walk on, images of the siege merge with others from a more distant time, impressed on my consciousness by the films of Eisenstein. Dark figures scatter across cobbles and tram tracks, fleeing bullets and mounted Cossacks. This sunny, crowded street was the epicentre of the 1917 revolution, the scene of the bread riots that sparked the events that changed the shape of the twentieth-century.

I turn off Nevsky onto Malaya Konyushennaya. Like the Anichkov Palace, the House of Youth Culture here is an after-school centre for children, now closed for the summer. The concierge leads me up a flight of stairs and into a sitting room. Its windows are swathed in muslin, insulation from the heat outside. An elderly man and woman are seated in armchairs. 'This is our former director, the dancer Madame Elizaveta Kulyagina, and this is Viktor...' I fail to catch his patronymic.

'I did fire watch duty,' says Madame Elizaveta. 'They tied a rope to my belt and lowered me down the slope of the roof. I grabbed the burning incendiary bombs with a pair of tongs and threw them off. I still have a scar where I was burned.

'And I worked in a factory making *katyusha* rockets. There were German prisoners of war there. We wondered what sort of people they were, how they could have waged war on us. They worked hard and well. During breaks they showed us photos of their mothers, wives and children. Sometimes they cried.'

I have seen newsreel shots of Leningraders shaking their fists at captured Germans being paraded down Nevsky. Guards had to form a wall to protect the prisoners from the wrath of local women. How Russian, I think, is this difference between public and private reactions towards the 'enemy'.

'The Germans suffered from Hitler too,' says Madame Elizaveta.

I walk over to a window. Pushing aside the curtain, I peer out. The sky is blue and clear where it was once clotted with barrage balloons.

Tourists wander across the cobbles, photographing each other. Behind them I see a ragged pile of corpses by the Griboyedov canal. My nausea returns.

'You adapt to the sight of death,' Madame Elizaveta's voice rings out behind me. 'When you know there is no way out and you can't run away you become resigned to the situation; you do not despair.'

She gestures for me to sit down in a chair beside her. 'Of fifteen children in our communal flat at the start of the war I was the only one to survive. My brother died; my father foretold his own death. He said he had lived through revolution, civil war and famine, but he would not survive this apocalypse.'

My shoulders slump beneath the weight of siege memory.

'But you see,' Madame Elizaveta slaps her palm down on the arm of her chair, 'I was always convinced that we would win. Just before the war my grandfather said, "The Red Cockerel will defeat the White Cockerel." I asked him what he meant. He replied, "I am speaking about Russia, holy Mother Russia. We shall win whatever happens." That thought comforted me; it kept me going until the last days of the war. My youth helped too.' She shakes her head. 'But I do not understand life today.'

'Everything is so different from before,' says Viktor. 'We lived without money.'

'We sewed our own costumes. We made skirts from trousers.'

'They were splendid costumes.'

'You see,' Madame Elizaveta leans forward confiden-tially, 'certain principles were instilled in us then. We try to retain them, to pass them on to the next generation. Young people do not place enough value on creativity. Everything today is about money.'

'That is not the most important thing, not important at all.' They shake their heads. 'Here we welcome all children – addicts, anyone. We have found needles in the toilets. We turn no one away. We learned you see, of the importance of finding one's creativity. It is the path to self-esteem.'

I make my way home down Nevsky. A sudden impulse propels me through the wood and glass doors of the House of Books. Upstairs I find a counter display-ing notebooks. There are no assistants in sight. I wander among deserted counters until I come across a girl drowsing behind a display of pens.

'I would like to buy a notebook.'

Without raising her eyes she nods her head in the direction I have come.

'There is no one working on that counter,' I persist. 'Can you help me?'

'No.' The word emerges as a prolonged sigh.

In Soviet days shop assistants were demi-gods to be placated and cultivated. Their goodwill was your conduit to scarce consumer goods. They could even provide you with mysterious items rarely seen on shop counters.

Further down Nevsky I find a kiosk piled with boxes of chocolate, bottles of liqueurs and plastic toys. I ask the assistant if she has such a thing as a notebook. She produces a school exercise book, its pages squared off. I request a pen too, and pay with an inflated sense of triumph.

I reach Lena's flat exhausted. My eye lids droop, I long to lie down, but I battle this fatigue.

To reach the icy Neva with one's bucket took a thousand tiny steps. A *blokadnitsa* would first have to conquer her morning weakness, raise herself from her bed, lower her feet to the floor, pull on one boot, then the other. Usually her fingers would be too frozen to move individually, so she had to pick up her boots using her two hands like stumps. She then had to raise herself to her feet, walk to the door without falling, hook her arm around the banister, take each stair carefully, one at a time. The steps would be sheeted with ice where neighbours' buckets had spilled. One slip could mean the end. She could not waste her energy on thoughts of the return journey, on anxiety over how she would get back up the stairs with a full bucket. In any case, she might never return.

I urge myself to attempt one word, and then a sentence, a paragraph… Slowly the words take shape on the page.

❧

A tram outside the flat is bombed. I help to pick out shards of glass from passengers' flesh, my arms steeped in blood. Upon awakening the dream lingers as an insistent, horrifying shadow, like that of a Messerschmitt in a cloudless sky. As I toss about on the divan my limbs become entangled in the sheet. This invokes such an unpleasant association with siege corpses that I get up and dress quickly.

I leave the flat, hoping that sunlight will drive the horror from my mind. But on the street I am paranoid, jumpy in the rush of traffic and pedestrians. I trip over the kerb. A hand shoots out to grab my arm. Bloodshot eyes meet mine. 'Where are you going, lady? What, American are you?' I break free and push through the doors of the metro.

Lena promised to meet me at the Hermitage. Dodging the tourist queues, I go straight to the education department. Svetlana frowns as I sink into a chair. 'You look tired.'

'She is having nightmares,' announces Lena who enters just behind me.

'Come with me,' says Svetlana.

But I only want to be left alone, to spend the afternoon drinking tea behind these thick walls, protected from the heat and the crowds. Lena and Svetlana are leading me along dark passageways. My legs tremble. I put a hand to the wall to steady myself. This visit was a mistake. I'll make an excuse, return another day. Strong fingers encircle my wrist. 'Come on, they are waiting for us.'

At the end of the corridor a young guide rises from her chair. She unlocks a door and ushers us through an air-conditioned foyer. The guide hands us mohair shawls as protection from the sudden chill. We step into an ancient kingdom of gold: Greek necklaces, headdresses and earrings so intricate they have to be viewed through a magnifying glass. And then I am lifted and taken far beyond the city to an even older, prehistoric world: gold amulets of deer with curly antlers, trees of life connecting earth to heaven, soaring women with fishtail wings and emerald eyes.

These are fluid Scythian shapes, magical amulets lifted from burial mounds on the southern steppes. Fifty years ago they returned to the earth, this time to the Ural mountains for the duration of the war.

'God-given light,' murmurs Lena. 'Those artists absorbed it and transformed it, reflecting it back out from themselves.'

Outside we stop to sit in the Admiralty Gardens. Around us children play tag on the grass in the shadow of the Bronze Horseman; their mothers chat on benches. A little way off, near the Hermitage a bear dances medievally on a chain.

A tramp in Wellington boots and a cardboard crown shuffles along the path towards us. He wears a threadbare naval jacket with gold anchors on the sleeves and carries a trident. No one takes any notice of him. Neptune stops to stare at me; I study the dome of St Isaac's. He waits. I submit. Catching his eye, I smile. Laughter bubbles up and bursts from my throat. He raises his trident in salute and then trudges on through oblivious crowds disgorging from their coaches in Admiralty Square.

12

A person who laughs is unvanquished.
Yevgenii Lind

It is night and Lena is asleep. I return to Boldyrev. To the place I left three weeks ago: *In one district mortuary 650–700 corpses arrive each day. Many, many of them have been chopped up, shredded.* A driver who delivers the dead tells him that at first the mortuaries did not hide children's bodies. But many were stolen during the night. Children's flesh was considered to be the most easily digested. *People would approach the lorries and ask for the children. Now they are locked away…*

'I have already told you that the publication of his diary was not met with universal enthusiasm,' Lena says in the morning. She hands me a slip of paper with an address. 'Aunt Nadya left this for you. She has managed to contact Yevgenii Lind. He is director of a museum dedicated to the work of artists and performers during the siege. It's called *The Muses Did Not Fall Silent*. It's closed at present for renovation but he'll see you tomorrow afternoon. He is the person to talk to. He knows everyone.'

The walls of Lind's room are papered with photos, festooned with orders and medals.

'My father was director of the Leningrad children's theatre before the war. He was killed at the front. I opened the museum on 16 March 1968, on the anniversary of his death.'

We sit down, facing each other across the room. His eyes meet mine. 'Do you know what dystrophy means?'

He tells me anyway. 'In the process of starvation the body eats itself. It breaks down the cells for protein. First the fat, then the muscle, then the organs. There is a point from which there is no return. When Abramov dropped dead on stage the audience thought he was acting and cheered.'

Trams rattle along the street outside. Waves of heat swirl through the open window. My mouth is dry, my eyes sting from dust.

'The Germans thought that our surrender would just be a matter of time. In November 1941, when they took the town of Tikhvin and closed their circle around the city we only had three weeks of supplies left. They had burned the Badayev food stores; they knew that we would soon starve.'

He snorts. 'Imagine how they must have felt when they heard our Radio Committee orchestra performing Beethoven's Ninth Symphony. It was broadcast live on 9 November 1941. The conductor was Karl Ilych Eliasberg, a Jew. A choir of 120 singers and the great soloist Sophia Preobrazhenskaya sang. The Germans heard it in their trenches. It so shocked them that some even gave themselves up.

'One of the cellists, a man called Brik, had his fingers burned in an incendiary bomb attack. Nevertheless he played till the end.' Lind's arm saws the air.

'Karl Ilych Eliasberg was one of the foremost conductors in the world, a priority target for the Germans. After he conducted Beethoven's Ninth they sent him a message of thanks for an *excellent performance of German music*. Signed by Dr Goebbels.

'But the orchestra suffered. Many members died of starvation or were sent to the front. As winter wore on, Babushkin – the Radio Committee's artistic director – decided to resurrect it. He announced over the radio that they were looking for musicians and that they would receive a slight supplement to their rations. Now that was no small thing. It could mean the difference between life and death.

'The first rehearsal was on 5 March. The cellists were lucky – they could wear heavy overcoats. The violinists had to wear thinner clothing to allow flexibility.

'By the 5 April they were ready to perform in the Pushkin theatre, whose walls were very thick. It was the coldest April for a hundred years – minus six degrees in the auditorium, yet Shmirova performed a Spanish dance in décolleté. They put on that concert for the workers who cleared corpses from the streets.'

In his excitement Lind's words spill out so fast that I struggle to keep up. 'You know that Dmitri Dmitrich Shostakovich composed his Seventh, the 'Leningrad symphony', for us. He had been evacuated from the city and the score had to be flown in. The conductor, Karl Ilych Eliasberg, saved his last potato so that he could starch his shirt for the rehearsal.

Dmitri Dmitrich would not have known that there was virtually no orchestra left by that time. Those that were left, including Karl Ilych, were dystrophic. Some of the musicians were too weak to walk to rehearsals – they had to be pulled on sledges.

'The premiere took place on 9 August 1942. It was a huge moral victory – unbelievable.'

Lind talks on through the afternoon, describing artists singing and playing at the front, at hospitals and factories, of poets reading to troops, of an army ensemble playing Tchaikovsky in a minefield beside Pushkin's grave, of soldiers sitting on newspaper in the aisles of the Musical Comedy theatre, of composers writing scores, of men and women wrapped in overcoats hunched over books in the city's central library.

'Actors went on stage at the Musical Comedy having eaten no more than 200 grammes of bread. Almost all the male actors died. Men died more quickly than women. There was a mortuary to the right of the theatre entrance. Yet they carried on. When they saw how the audience responded they redoubled their efforts.'

Lind bounces on his seat with schoolboy energy. 'That was our fight against fascism. I think it was Cervantes who said that 'the town opens its gates when the last defender dies.' No one ever entered our city as conqueror.

'With the passage of time people will realise what true heroes these *blokadniki* were. You sometimes hear it said that they were heroes because they had no choice.'

'But they did have a choice.' Whatever else, they had that.

'Exactly. They could have lain down and died.' He leans forward and speaks with heavy emphasis. 'Without their spiritual strength, a strength that went beyond words, this city would not have survived. Imagine a person, half dead from hunger, walking off the frozen street into a place where chandeliers blaze, where there is music and laughter. A person who laughs is unvanquished.'

13

My father organised some of the factory lads into
a musical group. They said it was that which more
than anything else helped them survive the siege.
They would hardly let him leave to go home at night.
Pavel Smirnov – band leader

'What is your name and where do you come from?'
An elderly woman sits before me, her face framed
by a mass of aubergine hair.

'Who are you working for?'

'No one.'

'Who is financing you? No, don't take notes.'

The siege bred exceptionally formidable women.

'I have a whole corpus behind me!' Tatiana Nikolaevna
tosses her mane and smiles, appearing suddenly girlish.

'She is letting you know who's in charge,' Lena
explains later, 'just so you understand there won't be any
funny business.'

The gates of the Palace courtyard open and an elderly trio enter, Tatiana striding in the lead. A tiny delicate woman and a man with the erect bearing of a soldier follow. He holds out his hand. 'Tikhvinskii, Svet Borisovich. I would like to present my gymnastic squad. We all trained together during the siege. Tatiana Nikolaevna you already know, and here is Lidiya Ivanovna.'

We shake hands.

'We still keep in touch to this day.'

The Professor leads us up a flight of stairs and opens a door off the landing. The room is occupied by a group of women who are obviously in the middle of a meeting. They look up, surprise and irritation on their faces.

The Professor steps forward. 'Who is in charge here?'

'I am,' says one. 'This is a staff meeting. We'll be leaving in two minutes.'

'What time do you make it?'

'Three-thirteen,' she replies.

'By my watch it is three-fifteen exactly. I have an appointment now with this Englishwoman.'

The teacher catches my eye. Suppressing a smile, she rises. 'Follow me!' She marches down the corridor, produces a key with a flourish and unlocks a room. 'Please…' Inside is a round table and several chairs. A breeze plays through an open window. The Professor hesitates.

'This is a much better room,' I assure him. 'An excellent place for our meeting.'

Mollified, the Professor snaps open his briefcase, extracts some papers and arranges them carefully on the table.

'Ladies first,' says the Professor.

Tatiana Nikolaevna takes out a notebook from her briefcase and clears her throat.

'My name is Tatiana Nikolaevna Chertkova,' she

announces, as though speaking to a packed hall. 'My parents were of peasant origin. My mother was a housewife and my father a builder. He was awarded a medal for his part in laying an electric cable under Lake Ladoga.' Her face softens. 'It was the values that my parents instilled in me that enabled me to live through the siege. At home we divided our bread between us. We could never consciously take anything if it involved hurting someone else.'

'That's right,' adds the tiny, frail, Lidiya Ivanovna in a whisper. 'Sometimes at the bakers emaciated old people held out pieces of bread to us children, but we never took anything that didn't belong to us. It was only a short step over that line but we never crossed it.

'I remember one day I came across a building that had just been bombed. On Chernyshevsky. It didn't have a proper concrete shelter, just an ordinary basement. The house had collapsed, burying those inside. A soldier stood by the ruin, covering his face with his hands. "They're all dead!" he wept. Then he noticed me. "Here, girl, take this bread." He offered me three loaves, two white and one brown. "What if someone comes out alive," I asked. "What will they eat?" He just shrugged and shook his head in despair. I took only one loaf.'

'You asked about our moral state,' says Tatiana. 'Well, those were the human values that enabled us to live through the siege. They were the values instilled in us by our parents and teachers.'

Professor Tikhvinskii has been waiting his turn. 'You asked me a question about the siege.' He speaks in a quiet, emphatic voice. 'Well, I can tell you that above all it made me a grateful person. Without the army and the Palace of Pioneers I would have died.'

He hands me a photograph of himself as a young

man. I look into an intelligent, sensitive face with wounded eyes. The same expression as today's, only now the skin has slackened, the mouth tightened and the crease between the brows deepened.

'You must have been young when war broke out,' I say.

'I was twelve, living on the Vyborg Side, an area of goods yards, warehouses and heavy industry. My parents were doctors, Party members. In 1941 they left for the front, with my older brother who was a pilot. I was alone, without family or close friends.' The Professor spreads his hands on the table and takes a deep breath. 'The stores my mother left soon ran out, the electricity was cut off and then the water.'

'What did you do?'

'I gathered lumps of coal from the railway line. I made wick and oil lamps to light my room. I went to the Neva for water. I slept on a metal bedstead with a board laid across it. I had one thin blanket for covering.'

I shudder. His eyes meet mine. 'I was used to austere conditions. I was brought up in a military family.

'I cut up my leather boots,' the Professor continues, 'boiled and ate them. I ate all the carpenter's glue in the house and then boiled sawdust. There was a vegetable warehouse in the neighbourhood. In the course of decades vegetables had rotted and formed a layer over the floor. I dug up that earth and ate it.'

'You survived on mud?'

'For a while. Then as winter approached I went to the army and asked them to take me in. I told them my father was a general and I didn't want to die. I said I was prepared to do anything, any work at all, if they would just let me live with them.'

'They agreed, even though my father was not a general but a colonel in the medical service. I stayed with them for a few months. In the end they sent me away to study. I left my comrades with tears in my eyes. Their parting words were, 'Lad, live for us, study for us.' Out of 900 men, only one returned from the war.'

'So you came here?'

'Yes.' He smiles and looks around the room. 'It was a miracle what they made out of this old dark building. I cycled here all the way from the Vyborg Side.'

'Every day?'

'There and back. Sometimes through shelling and artillery fire. I was very serious about my training. I became a gymnast, performing with my troupe in hospitals, schools and theatre halls. There was a strong sense of collectivism among us, which more than anything else helped me to survive.

'I was a Communist then,' the Professor continues. 'And I remain one today. I cannot betray my ideals. I joined the party in 1948; I have been a member for over fifty years. Like my parents before me, I live for society.'

'What happened to your family?' I ask the Professor.

'They returned safely from the war – my mother wearing a full chest of medals. My father had left home in 1939 to fight in the Finnish war. I had not seen him in seven years.' He permits himself a thin smile. 'I went down to the Moscow station to meet him. I recognised him from afar. He was walking towards me, talking to a comrade. I stopped, overcome by joy, preparing myself. He walked straight past me. How could I expect him to know me? I had been a child when he left. And how could I tell a man, especially in front of his friend, that he hasn't recognised his own son? I followed them. When the other man left I approached my father and we had a proper father and son reunion.' He clears his throat. 'Millions of children were deprived of that experience.

'In all honesty I can say I am proud of my life and work. I hold many honours, yet none of them are mine; they belong to my teachers, to those who encouraged me, who showed me the way.' He pauses for emphasis. 'The greatest reward is that we turned out to be useful people.'

The others murmur their agreement.

'And my friends, Tanichka, Lidiya... These are not only women but comrades. We lived through everything together. We have known each other for fifty-six years.'

'How did the siege affect your life afterwards?'

The Professor nods, as though anticipating the question. 'Let me give you an example. Two months ago I skied to the North Pole.' He speaks as lightly as if it had been a trip to the seaside. 'Our success in that expedition was due to outstanding organisation, self-discipline and mutual cooperation. For that I owe a debt of gratitude to the war. It accustomed me to front-line conditions, in which nothing is your own, you hold everything in common.

'Afterwards I visited some schools in Arctic towns and gave talks there about my experience.' He picks up a file and pulls out some sheets of squared paper that appear to have been torn from school exercise books.

'Yesterday I received some letters from the children who heard me speak. It's hard to read them, I get emotional...' For the first time the Professor's voice falters.

Tatiana Nikolaevna picks up the letters and reads out excerpts: '*What courage, I wish I had a granddad like him... It was amazing to meet such distinguished people; I can't put my feelings about it onto paper... Svet Borisovich is a great sportsman etc, etc.*'

'When I read the letters of those schoolchildren,'

the Professor resumes in a firmer tone, 'it means that I signify something to them as a person. In their eyes we have led extraordinary lives. We survived the war, we come from a different society. I am very happy that we are able to inspire young people with their whole lives ahead of them.'

His chest expands. 'I believe that we need human solidarity and spiritual inspiration, not only in the sense of following Christ's sermons but in building a strategy for the future. If we are able to raise our children as we ourselves were brought up, then all that we lived through will not have been in vain.'

He pulls his case towards him and snaps it shut. 'Life is an eternal conflict, a battle to overcome obstacles. Positive and negative emotions arise all the time – but within this it is possible to achieve an equilibrium.' He looks at me sternly. 'You do not achieve that equilibrium by doing nothing. We who have faced hunger and cold understand this.'

'Not all of us try to reach the North Pole,' says Tatiana.

'True, but we each have our own Everest to climb.' He rises from the table. 'Two days ago the director of our Arctic museum invited me to ski with him to the South Pole. It is a journey of 3,000 kilometres.' He squares his shoulders. 'I shall have to prepare myself.'

As we leave the Palace the Professor falls behind the others until he is level with me. He bends his head close to mine. 'Are you married?' he asks in a low voice.

'No.'

'We must do something about that. Come and visit me at home.' He hands me his card. 'Call whenever you like.'

A TV blares inside Aunt Nadya's cell. I knock on her door.

'Come in.'

She is reclining against plump pillows, legs outstretched on her bed. A black and white TV flickers on the window ledge.

'I met Professor Tikhvinskii this afternoon.'

'Mmm.' Her hand reaches for the open box of chocolates at her side.

The TV catches my eye. An old-fashioned British police car with flashing roof light squeals around a corner. Norman Wisdom shins up a ladder and falls into the arms of a waiting bobby. Aunt Nadya bursts out laughing.

'Delightful film,' she says as the credits begin to roll. 'You were saying?'

'The Professor made a profound impression on me.'

'Have a chocolate.' She holds out the box.

'Thank you. I don't think I've ever met a true Communist. Not in Russia, I mean.'

'They are in rather short supply,' adds Lena, who appears in the doorway behind me.

'They were murdered by Stalin in the thirties,' says Aunt Nadya. 'After that people joined the Party for the sake of their careers.'

'The Professor was abandoned when his parents went to the front. He learned to fend for himself.'

'Happened to a lot of us,' says Aunt Nadya.

'But I don't think he ever got over it. Now he travels to the North Pole – and to the South Pole next, that is his plan. At seventy.'

'And why not?' asks Aunt Nadya lightly.

'Maybe he's restless?' asks Lena. 'After what he's been through growing marrows on his allotment might be a bit tame.'

'He says extreme circumstances help him discover what he has inside himself.'

'Absolutely,' says Aunt Nadya. 'Look inside and throw out the rubbish. When normal circumstances are removed we are forced to become more authentic.' She crunches a praline.

I hesitate. 'I was a little surprised though, that you hold him in such high esteem, given that his world view is so different from yours...'

'He's a Communist you mean?'

'Well, yes.'

A purple moth flies into the room and hurls itself at the ceiling light. We listen to the frantic beat of wings on the bare bulb. Lena slides her hand up the wall and flicks the switch. Silence.

'Communism failed because it coerced.' Aunt Nadya's voice penetrates the gloom. 'But I respect Tikhvinskii. He demands from others a tenth of what he expects from himself. That is a rare quality.'

14

...And if I forget all else, let me remember
How, trembling in the wind
From the height of the fifth floor
A mirror hangs over the void
By some miracle it was not broken
People were killed, walls blown away –
It hangs, spared by blind fate
Above the precipice of grief and war
Witness to pre-war comfort,
On the damp-eroded wall
It preserves in its glassy depths
A woman's warm breath and smile...
From *Mirror*, Vadim Shefner 1942

As we lurch around a bend into the Haymarket I smell burning rubber.

'Something's on fire!' a passenger shouts.

The conductress stands beside me, counting off a fist-ful of dirty notes. 'Don't worry, it's only the brakes,' she yells back without raising her eyes.

The car fills with a brown haze.

'Smoke!' someone cries.

My heart pounds; there is an impenetrable barrier of women shoppers between me and the door.

Looking bored, the conductress elbows her way through the crowd and sticks her head into the driver's cab. The vehicle shudders to a halt and the driver alights, pretty in lipstick and bleached hair. A moment later she climbs aboard again. 'We'll make it!'

Act Russian, I urge myself. But at the next stop I jump up from my seat and burrow beneath sweaty armpits towards the door. I am the only passenger to alight, a mile short of my destination.

By the time I reach the address Lena gave me sweat has soaked my blouse. I press the bell and wait, arms clamped to my sides.

A voice pipes, 'Coming, coming…' Feet pad towards the door. It flies open. A small, round woman with a sweet face and white chignon ushers me inside. Nelly Pozner's tiny flat is immaculate and crammed with *objets*: lace fans, a gilt cherub candlestick, fragile porcelain vases. The scent of wax and floor polish pervades a room as ancient and cared-for as a country church.

'Let me first introduce you to my family.' She picks up a framed photograph of a slender blonde woman with Dietrich eyes. 'That's my beloved grandmother. She was voted Miss Krakow 1895. And here is my grandfather. His family threatened to disown him if he married her but he defied them and brought her to St Petersburg.

'My father was an actor; my mother a singer.' Nelly hands me a tin mirror painted with faded pink irises. 'This was her mirror. She took it to the front with her when she sang. It survived the whole siege.

'Oh! I forgot to introduce the most important members of my family – my plants. I talk to them all the time. Sometimes they get cross with me but today they are happy.'

Nelly takes me into a kitchen where Lena is already seated. The table is spread with a lace cloth and covered in cut glass dishes of salads. We were invited for tea. I should have remembered what that means.

Nelly piles blini onto our plates. 'Salad, caviar, take some more…'

'Thank you.'

She sits down. 'Well, you asked about the war. I was eight years old when it broke out and did not take it at all seriously.' She shakes her head. 'I thought war was just something boys played in the street. Only when Papa came home in a greatcoat smelling of sweat and tobacco instead of eau de Cologne did I sense that something had changed.' Her words tumble out with scarcely a pause for breath. 'I saw his rifle lying on their pink tulle bedspread – it was a horrible contrast.'

Lena leans an elbow on the table and rests her face on her palm. Her fork toys with the food on her plate.

'Things became very hard after Papa left,' says Nelly. 'The water was cut off. We had to go to the river with buckets and boil the water before we could drink it. One day my mother came back in tears without the bucket. She told me she had been bending over an ice hole in the Fontanka when she saw a human head beneath the water. In her horror she let go. After that she had to use a kettle. It only held two litres and emptied so quickly that Mamma would cry as she pulled on her felt boots again.'

With an effort, Lena collects herself and redirects her attention to our hostess. 'How did you survive?'

'Our furniture began to disappear,' says Nelly, 'and our clothes… We exchanged them for glue. It gave off a revolting smell as we heated it. Then we let it congeal into a sort of aspic which we ate with vinegar, mustard and bay leaves – we had these left over from before the war. It would damage your intestines if you ate it hot. The hardest part was waiting for the glue to cool down.

'Not long ago I was in a building that was being renovated. It was filled with a disgusting smell that turned out to be carpenters' glue. I wondered how we could have eaten it during the siege, but we did. Have some more courgette fritters?'

'Thank you. The sauce is delicious.'

'Sour cream, dill, sugar and gherkins.'

She hands me a fluted silver sauce boat.

'One day I was at the baker's with my mother. We collected our ration – 125 grammes for each of us – when suddenly a youth rushed up, knocked into my mother and snatched the bread from her hands. He ran off. Mamma cried out in her loud operatic voice. A patrol of soldiers was passing. They ran after the boy, caught him and brought him back to the shop. The boy had already sunk his teeth into the bread.

'I have never forgotten that boy's face.' Her voice catches. 'It was swollen and his eyes were expressionless, like those you see today in the faces of drug addicts, eyes that are no longer human.

'The soldiers asked my mother, "Was it him?" "No," she said, "It was not him." Thieves were shot on the spot.

'Perhaps it was already too late for the boy and the bread would not have saved him.'

'Your mother was quite well known, I believe,' says Lena.

'Oh yes. She sang on the radio, in hospitals and at the front. People used to comment on her beauty. But one night she came under fire as she sailed back from a concert in Kronstadt,' Nelly's voice trembles. 'A white streak appeared in the middle of her dark chestnut hair. She grew too thin for her beautiful velvet dress. Then she lost her nightingale voice.'

Tears fill her eyes. Lena's hand reaches across the table and folds over Nelly's.

'When the hunger became unbearable I would lie in bed and tell myself that one day there would be water and sweets and the cinema again. In my mind I would re-run all the shows I had seen at the children's theatre. Then I would revisit the palaces my grandmother had shown me before the war – Pavlovsk, Peterhof, Oranienbaum… I used to slide along their floors, through their galleries.'

'We all did as children.' Smiling, Lena turns to me. 'They gave you enormous felt overshoes to protect the parquet, and these were perfect for sliding when the guides weren't watching.'

Nelly begins to clear away the plates. I get up to help her. 'No, no, leave those.' She glances out of the window at the rosy sky. 'It is a lovely evening. Let's go for a walk. I'll show you my church.'

We walk down a street of late nineteenth-century terraces, porticoed mansions built for merchants and bankers. On the outside they retain the faces of Dresden or Prague, aged and crumbling, but still assured. Unlike Moscow or Samara there is no hint of Asia in this sombre street. Eight centuries ago when the Mongols invaded Russia, this borderland was no more than a tract of marsh. It was of no interest to anyone until Peter the Great arrived and viewed it through different eyes.

'When I lay in bed,' says Nelly, 'too weak to move, I had the most terrible feeling of being unneeded, redundant, useless. As I understand it, happiness is the sense of being wanted, of being of use to others.' She twists the gold chain at her throat. 'I am almost sixty-six years old and still in demand despite the fact that many people don't have work at all these days. But during the siege I suffered greatly because I felt I was of no use to anyone.'

'What is your profession?' I ask.

'I am a music teacher.' Her eyes light up. 'Music is my life. It is through music that one communicates with God. Recently I heard the nuns play church bells at Pskov. They make an unearthly sound. Rock music resonates with your sex organs, folk songs with your torso, classical music and romances with your heart, and Bach, bell-ringing and mantras with your spirit, with the cosmos.'

She is breathless now. 'Let's sit for a minute.' Slatted wooden benches line the street, occupied by a few pensioners enjoying the evening air.

The sky has turned a deep pink. Swifts wheel above the onion domes of the Church of the Transfiguration.

'Once the sight of a bird in flight was a miracle. They all died or flew away.'

'It is still miraculous; we just get used to it,' says Lena.

Nelly perches on the edge of the bench, excited now. She waves her hands as she speaks, charm bracelets jiggling on her doll-like wrist. 'This church remained open despite everything. Mamma used to come here to pray. When Papa left for the front Granny gave him an icon, although he was a Jew. She and my mother prayed over him. Papa took the icon and kept it in his pocket throughout the war. He never received a single wound. Since the war I have taken religion very seriously.'

'What happened to your family?' asks Lena.

'We began to find little pieces of bread hidden all over the flat. My grandmother said she was saving them for a rainy day. We knew then that it was too late for her. She died in February 1942. Afterwards Mamma wrote to Papa: *Goodbye my dear. Our house has been bombed: I've lost my voice. We are dying.*

'My father showed the letter to his commanding officer and was granted leave. When he reached our block of flats he hesitated, afraid to climb the stairs for fear of what he might find. A door opened above him and an old woman in a coat and headscarf emerged, carrying a kettle. Papa called up, "Tell me, Granny, is anyone in the Pozner family left alive?"

'That woman, my mother, threw herself into his arms. He couldn't bring himself to ask about me. "Don't worry, she's alive," Mamma reassured him.

'Papa had to carry me out of the house. I was too weak to walk. We were loaded into a lorry and driven across the Road of Life. It was already the end of March and the thaw had set in. Water seeped around the wheels. The lorry left its doors open so that we would have a chance to jump out if it began to sink through the melting ice.

'When we reached the mainland I kept shouting out, "Look! A cat! A dog! A living dog!" In Leningrad all the cats and dogs and even pigeons had been eaten.

'During our period of evacuation I formed a concert group with other children. We performed in hospitals. It gave me great joy to be able to do something for others – I no longer felt useless.

'We returned to the flat in 1945. It was empty. People had come in and taken our furniture. They probably thought we had died. Yet there was amazing honesty too. In 1945 we received a note from the laundry asking us to collect our linen. We had delivered it in 1941: two large bundles of sheets, my grandmother's pre-revolution tablecloth and three of my father's concert shirts. In 1945 these were incredible riches. The laundry workers could have exchanged our linen for bread.'

'The sad thing is that today such honesty appears astonishing,' says Lena.

'Then it was the norm,' says Nelly, brushing down her sleeves and straightening her cuffs. 'After our return I went to study at ballet school. I was so tiny and well-proportioned I earned the name "porcelain statuette". At the age of twelve I danced a solo role – a doll in *Sleeping Beauty* – at the Kirov.

'But then I contracted pneumonia and TB. The doctor said that only a miracle would save me. He didn't believe in miracles but the best thing I could do would be to give up ballet, leave Leningrad and eat good food. Otherwise I would not reach the age of sixteen. We went to my aunt's in Galitch but the landlady threw us out because I coughed so loudly I almost barked. In tears, Mamma went to a priest. He asked if I had been christened. She explained that her husband was a Jew and wouldn't allow it. The priest said, "He will forgive you. Let her be christened. Let her die a Christian." They christened me secretly, because it was forbidden, especially as I was a Young Pioneer.* The priest introduced us to a holy woman who made up a mixture of tallow, aloe, honey and badger fat – she reared badgers especially for this purpose. I had to eat that disgusting mess. My stomach turns at the memory. When I returned to Leningrad the following year the doctor looked at my x-rays and said a miracle had taken place. My lungs had opened up and I was out of danger.'

Nelly takes a deep breath. 'The war has made me value life more. Today I cannot bear to see ruined buildings. Even felled trees distress me. They are living things, after all.

---

*   The Young Pioneers was a Communist children's organisation, originally influenced by the Scouting movement.

'During the war I saw our city destroyed, and some years later I saw Dresden in ruins. I felt only compassion. I knew what they had gone through.

'And then shortly after my return my mother died. I was with her at the end. My memories of Dresden's Zwinger Palace – its beauty – helped me bear the grief.

'You see beauty and culture were our spiritual nourishment during the war, just as they are today. It is in our Petersburg genes.'

Lena smiles. 'That is certainly true.'

'You learn to transform your losses.' She beams. 'In the past I would only pray when things were bad, but these days I thank God for all my blessings.'

☀

'You are just in time for the tour.' They greet me in the Chinese Pavilion of the Oranienbaum Palace, just outside St Petersburg. It was the only one of Petersburg's outlying palaces to escape German occupation. Of course it is out of the question to tour the palace by oneself; it would probably never cross anyone's mind that a visitor might want to do so. I ask anyway.

'*Nel'zya.*'

Not allowed. The English word does not convey the finality of the Russian. In some circumstances it is a signal that a bribe is expected, but not here. I slip into a pair of felt overshoes and tag on to the group. We trail off in the wake of the dead voice of the guide. 'This style was very popular at the end of the eighteenth-century. It is called chin-oi-ser-ie…' I take out my notebook and pen. *Catherine the Great chased her courtiers through these rooms; Nelly Pozner and her grandmother walked here,*

Lena with her mother… This palace was the only one that
escaped occupation by the Nazis.

People are staring at me. I put my book away. A legacy
of spy mania or simply against the rules? The cloud
of unknowing…

I lag behind until the tired voice fades. There must
be a couple of rooms between us now. I slide my felt
shoes across the parquet. The walls of this room are
closely embroidered with translucent grey bugle
beads. Sunlight streams through tall windows. As I
slide the walls around me shimmer and melt, dissolv-
ing into the colour and substance of the Neva on a
June night.

I halt before an embroidered garden. Flowers and
pomegranate trees surround a golden pagoda. Birds of
paradise spread their wings and rise, curved tail feathers
whirring, pursuing butterflies across the opalescent sky.
This garden grew behind Nelly's closed lids when she
lay in her frozen room listening to bombs shatter the
city around her.

As I turn I bump into an elderly woman in a headscarf who has also lagged behind the tour group. She
holds a pair of opera glasses to her eyes. 'Such beauty,
such luxury. Just look how people lived then!'

Perhaps not everyone, but I don't want to dampen
her enthusiasm.

Outside the Pavilion the woman catches up with me.
She waves her opera glasses. 'I always bring these with
me to ensure I see every detail. Are you going this way?'
I nod, and we set off together through the park.

'It's my day off. I am retired, but of course I still work,
because my pension is not enough. Besides, I have to
support my daughter and granddaughter. And work
gives me something to do. I have two jobs.' She throws
me a sharp look. 'You are not from around here?'

'No, England.'

'And what is your profession?'

'I am a writer.'

'Ah, that is wonderful. And I am a teacher. Of physics.'

I glance at her face. She is old enough.

'People have been talking to me about the siege.'

My companion glances over her shoulder. Figures straggle up the path, following us out of the pavilion. To our right is a lake edged with lily pads. 'Shall we sit for a while?' the woman suggests, pointing to an iron bench overlooking the water. 'It will be cooler over there.'

Grasshoppers thwack against my bare legs as I follow her through the long grass.

'Well,' the woman says after we are seated. 'I was evacuated from Leningrad in time, with my parents. We went to Chelyabinsk in the Urals. The war was hard for us, but we didn't experience the hardest things. They wouldn't let my grandfather leave. He was a munitions worker. When we returned in 1944 he was dead.'

Turquoise dragonflies skim the surface of the water, their bodies iridescent in sunrays that have burst through the thunderclouds.

'We believed that he had been killed. He was a large, plump man, you see.'

I gaze into the canopy of chestnut branches above us. Heat-limpened leaves dangle over our heads like the feet of slaughtered chickens. Thunder rumbles in the distance.

'I heard that people who were starving sometimes lost their minds,' I venture.

'Oh it was not the starving.' She flicks her hand in dismissal. 'They might have eaten meat from a corpse but they would not have killed human beings for their flesh. They were too weak.' She leans closer to me and lowers her voice, although we are alone. 'There were those, on the other hand, who profited from the siege, from starvation. One of the neighbours in our communal flat was in the NKVD. They were strong and powerful people, without a conscience. There are people like that in every country.'

Scorched leaves rustle and swirl up from the path before us. A gust of wind silvers the lake.

'I guess there are,' I reply.

The wind gathers strength, flipping the edges of the lily pads, making them flutter like a thousand fans. Lightning flickers over the Gulf of Finland.

'Well.' The woman gets to her feet. 'I have enjoyed our talk. I'll leave you now. If you take the path to the right it will bring you to the gates. Turn left and you will reach the station.'

The canopy overhead darkens and begins to quiver. Leaves are spattered with pockmarks the size of kopeck coins. I rise and walk towards the park gates, raindrops freshening my skin.

I pass a row of houses with sagging wooden balconies. Women sit on walls under umbrellas, baskets of glistening berries beside them. Hungry now, I enter a café *Sport* with darkened glass windows. A naked woman writhes on a video screen. Young men with thick necks shout into mobile phones. 'Sportsmen' is the euphemism for thugs, enforcers and security guards. I should have known better.

I turn and walk out, heading back towards the station. Inside the concourse I follow the *Buffet* sign and find myself in a dining-room that could have been the setting for a Soviet *Brief Encounter*. Waitresses in cardboard caps serve scoops of beetroot salad and half-slices of black bread from a carved wooden counter. I take my tray and walk between cream-painted Corinthian columns to a table scored by countless *Sveta*s and *Slava*s. As I eat I inhale a cool, dank peppery smell, a remembered smell from childhood, from the era of coal fires and steam trains. But Petersburg trains are electric now. Steam has not run on this line for years, not since the war. Another hallucination perhaps, the whiff of some forgotten coal cellar, some relic of the siege.

15

Do you hear? The rain-soaked wind
Frisks in the gardens, waving boughs!
Do you recall, that in this world there are still
Wide horizons, roads, fields and ploughs?
Here in this city, which has no road out,
Here in this city, besieged now for years,
I see those liberated expanses
of Russian beauty, boundless, wild and dear
Olga Bergholtz

'The radio was the heartbeat of our city. It was the thread that connected one person to another. People listened to loudspeaker dishes in their flats. There were dishes on almost every street corner too. The radio broadcast air raid warnings and the all-clear signal as well as news and entertainment. When a programme was not being broadcast – and don't forget the announcers were starving too – they filled the silence with the tick of a metronome. That sound said, "We are still alive."

'Did it ever stop?'

'Once. On 8 January 1942 there was not enough

power to transmit. That silence was the most frightening thing of all. People found it intolerable. They feared it meant the end. They staggered through the snow to Radio House to find out what had happened. In a few days broadcasts resumed.'

Ludmila Grigorievna is an editor at Petersburg TV who has worked on siege documentaries. We talk in her office at the studios on the Petrograd Side. She tells me that her mother was working as an actress with Lenfilm when war broke out. 'She stayed, she survived the siege, but never acted again.'

Another life turned upside down, like Larisa, like Lena's mother, yet these women were among the fortunate.

'I call my mother every year on 27 January to congratulate her on the lifting of the siege.' Ludmila pauses. 'You know that the Musical Comedy remained open?'

'I heard.'

'Shows used to begin at four in the afternoon as bombing raids were less frequent between three and seven. Audiences went to the theatre hungry and sat in their felt boots and fur coats. They relished a bit of light and luxury, the décor, the costumes. It was medicine. When people were too weak to clap they bowed to the actors instead.'

She flushes with sudden animation. 'At first, when the air raid sirens sounded, soldiers in the audience would fire their guns into the air, encouraging people to run down to shelters. After a while they stopped bothering. If they were enjoying the performance the audience just shouted to the actors to continue.' She laughs. 'My mother told me that Porthos in *The Three Musketeers* had to lie down drunk. When someone stamped on his foot he had to say, "Who the devil is standing on my foot?" Each time he said this line the air raid siren went off. By the sixth attempt everyone was roaring with laughter. "Don't say those damned lines!" they cried. So he didn't and the sirens remained silent.

'We Russians think that when you have nothing left to lose then you can start to enjoy yourself, to let your hair down. I think you are more reserved.'

And I think that is an understatement.

Ludmila leans towards me, her voice urgent. 'Soldiers would watch a performance and then go directly to the front. Remember that where there is pain, where there is fear, when people sing and perform to you, your morale is raised, you are reminded that you have a huge country behind you. You are not alone.' Her fists clench. 'And you know that if you are killed then there will be others to step into your shoes. It is a subconscious understanding; it gives strength and meaning to your actions. And that is why these days in Afghanistan and Chechnya they send singers out to the troops, to show they are not abandoned or forgotten.'

After leaving Ludmila I wander through dusty streets to the botanical gardens on Apothecary Island. Hothouses of dark glass and rickety ironwork border an unkempt lawn. I throw myself onto the grass and close my eyes. Traffic rumbles in the distance. A thrush bursts into song and then falls silent. I lie still, feeling the beat of my heart inside my rib cage – a faint echo of the metronome that once pulsed through this city. These gardens helped to save the city, supplying vegetable seedlings to the allotments laid out in spring 1942. They also supplied medicinal herbs and digitalis to the hospitals, and nourished the spirits of the wounded with flowers.

'Your ticket?'

A peaked cap and holster are silhouetted against the sky. I sit up and scrabble in my bag. Damn this officialdom. I fish out a scrap of paper and hand it to the policeman.

'The tour group begins over there.' He gives me back the ticket and points to a pavilion by the entrance.

He is a young man. Perhaps he will understand.

'But I don't want to join a group. Can't I just stay here?'

'It is forbidden to lie on the grass.'

Act Russian. I get up and walk towards the pavilion, but just before reaching its entrance I duck behind a bush. Peering through narrow leaves I watch the policeman-shepherd's back recede across the lawn. To my right is a path overgrown with hogweed and clover. I follow it until I reach a chestnut grove. This side of the gardens borders the river. I sit down on an exposed root, hypnotised by electric eels of light writhing on the Neva.

Do what you like as long as you observe the outward form.

Ivan would have been pleased with me.

I find Lena at home on my return, her head buried in a pile of papers. I murmur a greeting and go to sit in the kitchen, out of her way. For the past few days she has been distant, caught up in work.

But she walks into the kitchen after me.

'Don't let me disturb you.'

'You're not. How did you get on today?'

I tell her about my meeting with Ludmila. She laughs when I repeat the story of Porthos.

'Our Dionysian element lies very close to the surface. In the west it is more deeply buried, or you are losing it. I can't tell which.'

Cornflowers stand in an empty kefir bottle, their dried petals scattered on the table. Lena's fingers work quickly, pinching them into little piles.

'But you see,' she says, 'some of us fear the wildness within ourselves. They think that once unleashed it will rage out of control. They project their fear onto others, believing that only force can rein it in.'

'Dictatorship?'

'Uh-huh. Democracy is a dirty word to many here. All those *babushki* on the bus, complaining about what's been pilfered from their allotments. They always hold the *demokrati* responsible, as though they were thieves in the night.

'I've heard the grumbles in the bread queue.'

Lena sweeps the petals into her cupped hand and stands up. 'People grew used to being taken care of from cradle to grave.' She opens the balcony door. 'They never learned to take responsibility for themselves. It's a vicious circle.' She releases the petals into the air. 'If you are treated as a child, you behave as a child. People complain about the government, but we don't want to be held accountable for our own actions.'

16

*For most Leningraders the object was not to find
ways of surviving but to find ways of living.*
Granin and Adamovich – Book of the Blockade

I cannot resist Chekhov Street. Shabbier than
Millionaire's Row, as yet uncolonised by the new rich,
its nineteenth-century mansions echo with the ghost
of Karenina. Wall plaques announce: *Here lived Glinka;
Sergei Esenin often visited; this house is built in the Russian
Mauretanian style...*

House number 3 is grand and forlorn, the grey-green
paint flaking from its walls. *1883.* Its entrance is guarded
by a stucco snake twisted around a sword; caryatids
clutching laurel garlands support the portico. A tall
sapling sprouts from a balcony.

An elderly woman in a faded housecoat emerges
from an archway at the side of the house and shuffles
across the road towards me.

'Excuse me for staring at your house,' I say. 'But it's
very striking. Have you lived there long?'

'All my life. It was built for a Dr Krayevsky – you

see the snake and the sword? After the revolution it was turned it into communal flats. Then in 1965 they modernised it. They ripped out our wood and mirrors.'

'It has survived a lot then.'

'It has. But now some foreigners are talking about evicting us and turning it into a private bank. Better it fall to ruins than that. We are fighting them.'

'I wish you luck.'

I hurry off, crossing a park to reach the Alexander Nevsky monastery. In its grounds lie the remains of Tchaikovsky, Borodin, Rimsky-Korsakov, Mussorgsky and Dostoevsky. According to legend in 1941 a winged man appeared among their graves, radiating light. When the police arrived he flew up to perch on a tombstone. 'Your bullets won't touch me; I'll fly down when it suits me,' he shouted when they threatened him. And then he uttered his final warning: 'A dark figure approaches. He carries a black cross. Hunger will grip you as he waits at the gates. Eat up your beans, prepare your coffins. Amen.' Then he flew away. That was the last that was ever seen of him.

Lena has arranged an appointment for me with a priest, Father Andrei. Conscious of my sweaty and dishevelled state, I splash my face under a tap in the ladies cloakroom in the monastery basement. As I straighten up I meet the eyes of a woman in a black headscarf. 'Why don't you wash your hair too?' she hisses. 'Right under the tap?' I stand mute, paralysed by the venom in her eyes. An unwitting heresy on my part or is she mad?

Shaken, I hurry through the lobby, past a row of seated petitioners, placid women in headscarves clutching slips of paper. I am directed upstairs to a narrow office. Father Andrei is middle-aged and vigorous, with a black beard and soft brown eyes. 'I am not a *blokadnik,*' he tells me. 'I was born in 1945. My grandfather owned several shops in Petersburg but lost them all in the revolution. My grandmother belonged to the old intellectual class. Most of her contemporaries were wiped out by Stalin during the purges of the 1930s. I wanted to be a drummer but my grandmother would not let me play in a band. It would have meant joining the Young Pioneers and she despised them as hooligans.'

'Did people start to go to church during the siege?'

He shakes his head. 'Don't think they suddenly turned to God because they were afraid of dying.'

A clumsy question. I am dull-witted today, my mind numbed by the relentless heat. I can't seem to express myself in any coherent fashion. The winged man hovers before me, impish, laughing at my confusion.

'Temptation,' whispers Lena's voice. 'Don't listen to it.'

'About ten churches were open,' Father Andrei continues. 'There was not a noticeable increase in attendance. It was mostly older people who went. Young men and women were at the front.'

I try again. 'How did anyone survive the siege?' I ask. 'I fear that faced with those circumstances I would have succumbed, my body would have given out.'

'Remember that people had families, colleagues.' His tone is patient. 'They struggled to survive for the sake of those around them. Even if their immediate family died they had friends, workmates…'

Send not to know for whom the bell tolls…

I relax, soothed by the kindness in the priest's voice.

'You see, the Christian view is that life is a gift from God. We struggle to preserve it. Remember that most people at the time had been brought up by parents who were believers.

'For a Christian the siege was not a separate part of life. It was just something else to be lived. Death lost its fear – look at people who work in hospices, they grow used to death. As for the bombs, people could tell by their whistle whether to run and take shelter or not.

'People even got used to the corpses, piled up every-where like the carcasses of pigs and cattle you see in butchers' vans. They couldn't do anything about the situation. It was a form of resignation.'

'Dostoevsky said,' I remark, 'I can't remember where, that the defining quality of a human being is that he or she can get used to anything.'

'Yes in a sense that is true. You get used to it but you must not accept it. No! You might get used to the sight, but when you step on a corpse because you haven't the strength to move around it, that you must not get used to. You must be aware of what you are doing. You must pray and ask its forgiveness. If you do not you are lost.'

※

Accordion notes draw me along the path. A group of elderly people are gathered around a bench in our court-yard. On tiptoe, I peer over their shoulders. A man in dark glasses is playing a folk tune. A woman begins to sing, a mournful Carpathian throat song. Another joins her.

A tall veteran with a chestful of medals catches my eye. He beckons. I hesitate. He holds out his hand.

'Come over here and be with the people. You want to, I can see it in your eyes.' I am enveloped in vodka breath.

'We shall never forget those summer nights…'

'You might have walked past. Now you have witnessed a marvel.' The veteran nods towards the accordionist. 'He is blind you know. He comes here every Saturday. No one pays him.'

A woman in a peasant blouse breaks away. Others follow. They spread across the road that runs through the middle of the housing estate, skirts billowing as they twirl. Old men in summer suits step up to take their hands.

A black Zhiguli weaves along the road, its driver on a mobile phone. The dancers fall back.

'Girls!' shouts the accordionist. 'If you let another one through I shall stop playing.'

They skip back to their places. Now a four-wheel drive with blackened windows approaches. It hoots. The engine revs. A door opens and a man in shades emerges, his mouth hurling inaudible curses into the music. He throws down his cigarette, slams the door, spins the car and roars off.

A plump woman in a fuchsia blouse and spandex leggings is by my side. 'Beautiful, aren't they?' She has the apple cheeks of a milkmaid on a Soviet poster.

'So is the music.'

'He is my husband. Come and say hello.' The accordionist has paused for a cigarette.

'This is my Pavel. And my name is Sveta. Pasha dear, we have a foreign guest with us.'

Long fingers probe the air, their tips tapping invisible keys. I place my palm beneath his. Catching my hand, he flips it over and presses it to his lips. 'Delighted.'

'I hear your music from our flat in the evenings. I am staying with my friend across the road. How did you learn to play?'

'Well, I lost my sight when I was a child, during the war...'

'In Leningrad?'

'No. We lived in occupied territory, to the west of the city. A German soldier used to give us chocolate. He told us he had a blind son. The SS shot that soldier.'

'After the war I used to listen to an orchestra play waltzes in the town square. The music made me cry.'

'Why did it make you cry, Pasha?' asks Sveta.

'Because it was sad. I wanted to play music like that. So I learned to play the accordion. When I grew up I went away to perform on pleasure boats. I met Sveta.' He reaches out. Her hand flies into his. 'In autumn she took me to play in the Arbat in Moscow. In spring we would return to the river.'

'You music gives us great pleasure.'

He picks up his instrument.

'Come and have tea with us tomorrow,' says Sveta. 'Bring your friend.'

The indomitable dancers step into the road again.

'This is the last generation who will dance here,' she says.

※

'Welcome!' Sveta opens the door and kisses each of us in turn. Her face creases with pleasure as I press a bunch of ruby peonies into her hands. She ushers us into a sunlit kitchen. Plates are laid out, laden with cake and sweets.

'Please sit down. I am sorry we do not have much to offer you today, I have only just got home from work. Pasha,' she calls out. 'Our guests are here. Will you play?'

A mumble from the living room. Sveta disappears.

'I'm sorry.' She returns to the table, her face solemn. 'Pasha asks to be excused. He says he does not feel like music this evening. Please forgive him.'

She pours tea from the samovar.

'How did you meet Pavel?' asks Lena.

'It was on a river boat on the Volga. A long time ago now. We sailed from Petersburg to Astrakhan. I was working as a waitress. I fell in love with his hands. I had never seen such expressive hands. When he finished playing that first night he got up and bumped into a wall. I thought he was drunk. It wasn't until I saw him the next day that I realised he was blind.

'It was spring. Nightingales sang along the river banks.' Sveta's cheeks glow rose. 'What more do you need?'

I remember those Volga nightingales too, how their song accompanied Ivan and me on our evening walks beside the river as we watched the sun sink behind the Zhigulevski hills. And the overpowering scent of honey, richer and sweeter than anything I had smelled in my life. I had asked Ivan what it was. 'Wild flowers,' he had replied, in disbelief that I had not known. 'What an impoverished place you come from,' he added.

17

Music illuminates a person and
provides him with his last hope
Dmitri Shostakovich

My fist pounds on the door, as instructed. It is opened by a woman in thick pink lipstick and a grey suit. Her dignified, slightly masculine glamour reminds me of Aunt Nadya.

'Where are the men?' she demands, glancing down the corridor.

'I am alone.'

'Oh.' Such disappointment in her voice. 'I thought you'd have a camera crew with you.'

For years Ksenia Makeanovna Matus toured the country giving talks. Cameras and journalists came to her flat – from Japan, Germany, France…

'But not any more.'

She shows me a photograph of her younger self in furs, black hair piled in a beehive. A row of medals on her breast, she bends to receive a bouquet from a group of Young Pioneers in Tashkent.

'Looking back, I don't understand how I survived the siege. Only through strength of character. I've seen everyone die over the years, family, school friends, colleagues, but I live on.'

'May I ask when you were born?'

'Guess!'

She's probably about eighty. 'Let's see, seventy-seven?'

'Eighty-three!'

We laugh.

I feel as though I have known Ksenia for a long time. She reminds me of my great aunts – women to whom convention was of no great importance.

'I was born in 1916, so that makes me how old when war began? You work it out. Maths was not my strong subject. Twenty-five? Yes. I was studying at the Conservatoire. I began with the piano and violin but went on to play the oboe. My training was interrupted by the outbreak of war.'

Ksenia pulls out a diary from the bookshelf and begins to read: '*Today we ate the last of the cabbage soup. Nothing remains for tomorrow. I have to go to the market to exchange something of value for sunflower seed husks to bake and grind into flour. You deceive yourself that you have eaten and will therefore survive a little longer...* Oh well, enough of that. It's not interesting.'

'Of course it's interesting.'

She brightens. 'Shall I read some more?'

'Yes, please.'

'*31 December 1941: A new year begins. All over the world people are celebrating but what can we in Leningrad hope for? No one knows. Perhaps each of us can expect to meet only death. How I long to go out into the deep countryside... to lie in a valley somewhere, in long grass and let the sun warm my frozen bones. I want to see space around me, so much space that the eye cannot take it all in at once. I want to listen to nature's music, the babble of a stream, birdsong, the rustle of grass; the enchanting music that no instrument can recreate. Oh, God, how much beauty there is in this world, only not in ours.'*

Ksenia Makeanovna looks up from the pages, 'What's the matter? Don't cry.' She smoothes the page before her. 'The diary helped me. There was no one to talk to. Shall I go on?'

'Please.'

'The city is collapsing, people are dying, and there is no way out. The cemeteries are full of the dead, you see an endless procession of bodies being pulled through the streets on sledges. Trams no longer run. There is no light in our flats; no wood for heating. People walk like corpses on swollen legs, their faces blackened from the cold. At first we had hope, now I can't imagine that we Leningraders shall ever return to life, even to a dreary and mundane existence.

What does a person need in this life? Only another 100 grammes of bread – and then what joy would shine in their eyes! They might even smile.

'So there we are. My brother and sister had gone to the front, my mother was in hospital, my friends were dead.

'In spring 1942 I heard a radio appeal for musicians. Shostakovich's Seventh Symphony was to be performed in Leningrad. When I went to the Radio Committee to register I found them exhausted, hungry and dirty. Smoke from wick lamps had blackened their faces. They registered me as second oboist. The first oboist was still downstairs, too weak to climb to the third floor. The conductor, Karl Ilych Eliasberg, asked if anyone could assist her. My friend and I went down. We helped her upstairs, supporting her under the arms.

'Karl Ilych gave us the date for the first rehearsal. I went home to look for my instrument. The stops had turned green and some had fallen off so I had to get it repaired. The instrument maker welcomed me. "Oh my dear, it is so good to see you. Sit down." I told him I wanted my oboe mended. He was delighted. On his bench lay a pile of fur which I took for a hat or a muff. "My cat," he said. "I have just eaten it."

Ksenia Makeanovna stubs out a *Belomor Canal papiros* – a cardboard tube with a plug of rough tobacco in one end. She started smoking these during the siege and has stuck to the brand all her life. 'They numbed the hunger pangs. Where was I?'

'The first rehearsal.'

'It was horrible. We lasted for fifteen minutes. We were all dystrophic.' A sharp glance. 'Do you know what dystrophy is?'

I nod.

'We couldn't even sit on our chairs; we rested on nothing but bones. Cushions had to be placed under us.'

She extracts another *Belomor* from the packet, pinching the cardboard tube to make a holder.

'It was only thanks to the character of Karl Ilych that we succeeded in performing the symphony at all. During rehearsal the first trumpet, a soloist, dropped his instrument onto his lap. "First trumpet, why aren't you playing?" asked Karl Ilych. "I'm sorry, I have no more strength." "Do you think any of us have?" Karl Ilych replied. "Pick up your instrument." The man lifted his trumpet and resumed.'

Ksenia pauses. 'Do you know the date of the performance?'

'9 August 1942.'

'Correct! It was a cold summer. The concert hall was freezing, but as soon as I stepped onto the stage I felt revived. Neither hunger nor cold would kill me. I would survive.

'The public arrived. Most of the men were in uniform. We musicians wore warm underwear beneath our outer clothes. The men in the wind section wore gloves with cut-away fingers. We were all dystrophic.

'That symphony touched us deeply. Afterwards the audience gave us a long standing ovation. We stood and bowed to them. Then we hugged each other. Tears ran down our faces.

'General Govorov, commander of Leningrad forces, was there. Afterwards Karl Ilych thanked him for coming. "Well I assisted in the performance too," the General replied. "We ordered our batteries to fire on all the German positions and continue firing, so that the performance would not be interrupted. We gave them a symphony they won't forget."

'9 August made a great difference. The shelling and bombing and hunger continued but I knew I had accomplished an important deed, that I was of use to the city. Those excerpts I read from my diary, they convey a sense of uselessness, don't they?'

I nod.

'Well, playing the Seventh changed all that. On 22 June of this year the Philarmonia played it again. I was invited; they sent a car for me. There are only three original performers in Petersburg and one was too ill to attend. It was a splendid occasion. The public gave us a standing ovation. We were presented with beautiful bouquets and boxes of food that I could never dream of buying. Afterwards they interviewed us. All the same, it was painful to listen to that music, to return to the past.

'I stayed with the orchestra during the war and afterwards, until I retired in 1985. On the day I left the orchestra I thought my life was over.

'My husband had been a violinist. When we sat

together at home he would call me over to the radio. 'Listen, Keshinka, our orchestra is playing.' But it hurt too much to listen.

'I had nothing to do but look after my granddaughter. She plays the piano very well. I helped to teach her.'

I glance at the instrument standing against the wall. 'Does she play it still?'

Ksenia shakes her head. 'Not here. She is in America now. They were only going for a month but they have stayed. Dasha has a boyfriend there, she gives concerts…'

'Why don't you go over to visit her?'

'What, at my age?'

'It's possible.'

'For healthy people perhaps, but I have already had a heart attack. And high blood pressure. I fell over on the ice last winter and broke my foot. I am afraid to go out alone now.

'These days I sew.' She picks up a cushion from the sofa. Embroidered violets on pale gold satin. 'And this one.' Yellow chrysanthemums on pink.

Ksenia pulls at my loose summer dress to show where I should make tucks. 'To show off your bust.'

I laugh.

'But why hide your beauty? Are you married?'

'No.'

'Oh, I wish that you could find a husband. So you won't be lonely.'

As I leave I pass a side table near the door, set with miniature cups and saucers. A collection of dolls is seated around it.

'We used to hold tea parties together,' says Ksenia Makeanovna, 'when she was little, with her dolls.'

The backs of our red plush seats curve in a gentle rhythm that harmonises with the smooth white arches above our heads. Aunt Nadya, Lena and I are in the front row of the Philarmonia balcony. Dmitri Shostakovich's son Maxim is conducting. He bows to the audience, then turns, lifts his baton and begins to draw notes from the orchestra. They rise and pour outwards across the city, as they once did across shattered Europe. Behind closed lids I see my grandparents gathered around wireless sets, cocooned by blackout curtains, listening to the music of a city they had believed to be dead.

The auditorium is filled with men in uniform and ladies in freshly-cleaned coats. One of them dares to wear pink. Ksenia sits at the side of the stage, her cheeks hollow, oboe to her lips. The music is angry, tender, triumphant. The last notes die away; a deathly hush fills the hall. They are on their feet now, applauding, tears streaming down their cheeks. A small girl with a huge white bow in her hair totters up the aisle with a bouquet and presents it to the conductor. His emaciated figure bends to receive it. The musicians rise from their seats, unsteady on thin legs. They bow to the audience, and then turn to embrace each other.

The fat man beside me is on his feet, squashing his belly against the balcony rail as he leans out to applaud. 'Bravo!'

'Are you ready?' Aunt Nadya is tugging my arm. 'Let's go.'

I drift along in her wake, thinking of Ksenia.

'She was fun,' I say.

Aunt Nadya snorts. 'What did you expect?'

18

You stand before me, Leningrad.
I uncover the golden spire
and resurrect your finery.
Olga Firsovna 1945

A fit of coughing pulls me from a dream. Smoke. I leap out of bed and dash into the kitchen. The cooker is switched off. I open the balcony door. The apartment block opposite gleams dully through a brown haze.

A muffled voice asks, 'What are you doing out there?'

'There's a fire.'

'What? Oh that. It's not in the city, it's the forest outside. I heard it on the news. Don't worry. Go back to sleep.'

But I am transfixed by the red glow on the horizon, as though this were the night of 8 September 1941 and I was watching the Badayev food stores burn.

'It is an omen,' remarks a passenger on the tram.

'I heard there will be floods across Europe.' Her companion shakes her head.

'We will have an earthquake at the end of August.' The first Cassandra folds her arms in satisfaction.

I am on my way to meet another siege legend. In 1941 Olga Firsovna scaled the Admiralty spire to tie camouflage material around it. As much a Petersburg landmark as the Statue of Liberty is to New York, it was feared that German bombers would use the spire as a navigational aid.

Aunt Nadya has given me the address of a café in a south western suburb. I am relieved that it is on the gulf side of the city, away from the forest.

The appointed café is on the ground floor of a monumental Stalin-gothic block. I arrive early. The place is empty. The waiters vanish. Used to Russian cafés by now, I sit down at a pavement table and open the book I have brought with me.

Guardian Angels shows a photograph of a woman in shorts, holding a rope, her bare legs braced against the Admiralty spire, high above the city. A colleague has risen in a balloon anchored to the ground to attach the rope.

A short woman limps across the road on the arm of a younger companion. She wears a smart suit and a beret on her bobbed hair.

'Caroline? This is my daughter, Olya.'

Olga Afanasyevna settles herself at the table. She glances over her shoulder. A young waiter materialises.

'What's your name?' She smiles up at him.

'Andrei,' he whispers to the floor.

'Andryusha, a glass of wine for me and two coffees for these ladies.'

Against my expectations Andrei returns quickly with the correct orders.

'I am not impressed by the new Russia.' Olga takes a swig of wine. 'This perestroika is just an experiment. I shan't vote in the elections – there's no one worth voting for – but if the Communists get in again I'll shoot them. Personally. Most of my friends have emigrated to Israel, Germany or America.'

Olga is ninety years old. She was born in Switzerland to Russian parents.

'In 1905 my parents went to Switzerland to study. Ten years later they were offered Swiss citizenship but they refused and returned to Russia. My father was shot during Stalin's repression and my mother died during the siege.

'My father had a very strong influence on me as a child. Even when he was not around we heard his words, his voice. We always obeyed him. He taught me to take risks. In the summer of 1925, when I was sixteen, he took me to the Crimea. We walked from Sebastopol to Alushta, climbing all the peaks on the way.'

Ivan introduced me to that indomitable landscape; we took a trip down there together. He said the Crimea was the most beautiful place he had ever seen. We walked among cypresses and hibiscus, admiring moths the size of humming-birds. We climbed hill-sides to gaze out over a dolphin-flecked sea. Alushta was as charming as old-fashioned Brighton but Ivan complained about the plumbing. I doubt that would have bothered Olga.

'That summer I fell in love with mountains,' she says. 'Later, in the holidays, my husband and I would go to the Caucasus to work as climbing instructors.

'Once when I was giving a talk about climbing the spire a young boy said to me, "You are a living relic." I was furious, but I understood that people today simply have no idea, they cannot imagine what it was like.'

Olga extracts a cigarette from her packet. She leans into the open window behind her and calls out, 'Andryusha, a light!'

Andrei emerges with a box of matches. He blushes as she beams her thanks.

Olya tells me she works for a foreign company. 'I used to be an interpreter to the manager of a large metal works. But I couldn't stand the corruption. The bosses took everything while the people who did the real work went unpaid.'

A familiar story. When I lived in Samara during the era of 'shock therapy', I witnessed the enrichment of a few, like Ivan, and a virtual return to the barter economy for the rest. Wages for industrial workers, teachers and office staff went unpaid for months. Savings were wiped out by inflation. Once again, Russians survived by cultivating their allotments and bartering goods when they were paid in kind. Friends complained of a shift in mentality, that selfishness had taken hold, and for the first time in living memory there were thefts from allotments.

In the spring of 1942 allotments were dug in the parks and squares of Leningrad – often planted with little signs bearing the owner's name. No one stole from those allotments.

Olga finishes her wine. 'Strange things happened to me during the siege. One day I was on the street desperately looking for food. I tried to barter a skirt but no one wanted it. I was terrified of going home to my mother empty-handed. Suddenly I felt something beneath my foot, lying under the snow. I found a lump of frozen bread – a whole ration. I did not ask myself who had lost it – there was nothing I could do. My strength came flooding back as I took it home to thaw out.'

'One morning I was walking down Nevsky when the sirens went off. The air raid wardens grabbed me and pushed me into a shelter at Gostinny Dvor. I was annoyed and wished they'd left me alone. Sometimes you just wanted to go on your way. Especially if you were on your way to the canteen.

'A bomb hit the street and blocked the entrance, burying everyone inside. A sewer was shattered; the liquid began to rise and flood the shelter. It was pitch dark. I waded through the sewage, stumbling over corpses, until I came to the wall. There I found a ledge and climbed onto it. The sewage kept on rising until it reached my knees. I feared the fumes would suffocate me.' Olga picks up her glass and drains it. 'Fortunately I have always had a good sense of smell. I detected a stream of fresher air somewhere above my head. I stood on that ledge for hours without moving, gasping at that air, praying that the sewage wouldn't rise any higher. Finally I heard shouting. I called back. A hole opened above my head. Rescuers pulled out the living and the dead. Someone tried to wrap a coat around my shoulders but I shook it off and walked straight home across the river to the Petrograd side. By the time I reached home it was night.

'After that experience, eating cats seemed like a luxury. And people in England say, "Oh yes we suffered too during the war – it was hard to get butter."'

Olga stubs out her cigarette and gets to her feet. 'To what do I attribute my survival? I don't know myself. I guess it's in my genes.'

They take their leave while I linger at the table. Their receding figures are swallowed by a noisy group of teenage girls making their way down the street. *I've got the looks and you've got the money* is emblazoned in sequins across the chest of the loudest girl.

The front door swings open before I can put my key in the lock. A blow knocks me aside. Winded, I clutch at the door frame for support. A chill of panic runs through me. A robber? Turning, I glimpse a slight figure with long legs teetering down the corridor on spike heels. An unlikely burglar.

Rubbing my bruised arm, I cross the threshold and slip out of my outdoor shoes. I find Lena and Aunt Nadya in the living room surrounded by piles of clothes. I pick up a sheer blouse stamped with yellow flowers. *Made in Turkey*.

'Not quite your style,' I remark, still ruffled by my encounter at the door.

Lena snatches the blouse from my hand and throws it back onto the pile. 'Don't be silly.' She colours.

'These are not for Lena, obviously,' says Aunt Nadya. 'An importer brought them. She just left.'

'Why, are you going into business then?' I stare at them both in surprise.

'Not exactly.' Lena mumbles, avoiding my eyes. 'I can sell these through Naima Suleimanova. She is very well connected.'

'In that respect at least,' Aunt Nadya murmurs.

'I don't get it.'

'You see, the girl wants her sister to enter the college where I teach.'

The penny drops. 'You've taken a bribe.'

'Not a bribe,' they say in unison. 'A gift.'

I was naïve in imagining Lena and her aunt to be somehow beyond the Russian system of favours. It is the oil that greases the machine and to me, the most complex and mystifying aspect of life here. Without connections or *blat* you are a non-person; you scarcely exist. *Blat* renders the impossible possible. Haven't made the grades for university? No problem. A word to the admissions staff and they will tell you what they need.

And so it goes on, from the Kremlin to the Gulag, where the criminal underworld developed *blatnoi*, a cant that derives many words from Yiddish.

Lena flops down amongst the clothes. 'It is humiliating. My friends and I ask ourselves how we can engage in business. In Soviet days trade was a criminal offence. And I still have difficulty... I wasn't brought up for it. Yet the college only pays me $50 a month.' She points at her aunt. 'It's her. She's the one who got me into it.'

'Doesn't bother me.' Aunt Nadya shrugs. 'We traded during the siege. *Speculators,* we were called. You can't imagine what a filthy word that was to the Soviet mind. At first the police broke us up. Raided the markets. But in the end they were forced to turn a blind eye. They were at it themselves of course. We sold everything. We had no choice.'

'But we are no longer besieged,' says Lena, turning to me. 'For me business means gangsters.'

She gets to her feet and goes out to the kitchen.

She never approved of Ivan. Or rather, the idea of him. They never met, but I heard the reserve in her voice when I spoke about him on the phone. Which is hardly surprising, given her suspicion of business. The chasm that exists between the intelligentsia and the new breed of *biznesmenov* echoes that between the pre-revolution elite and the Communist masters who replaced them. Despite selling books on the street to pay her rent, Lena never lost her sense of moral superiority. I can picture her lording it over her alcoholic *komunalka* in the manner of an exiled white Russian countess presiding over a Parisian dosshouse.

'She'll learn.' Aunt Nadya interrupts my thoughts. 'Actually it's interesting to put yourself to the test.' She pushes aside a pile of rhinestone-studded jeans. 'I'll be glad to get this *schmotki* out of the flat.'

My ears prick up. *Schmotki, schmutter*... 'You speak *blatnoi*?'

Her glance is withering. 'With so many of my friends in camps over the years – *zeks* *- I should think so.'

---

*   *Zek* – shortened form of *zaklyuchonii*: prisoner, inmate of the Gulag.

19

Woman of Leningrad! ... Everywhere and everything
bears the traces of your lovely, capable and faithful hands.
You are at your factory bench, at the bedside of the
wounded soldier, on fire watch, in institutions, at schools,
children's homes and nurseries, behind the wheels of cars,
chopping wood, loading barges, your clothes are those
of the working woman, police officer, air raid warden,
railway worker, army doctor, telegraphist. Your voice is
heard on the radio, your hands till the soil of allotments
throughout Leningrad, in all her gardens, parks and
squares. You guard our buildings, you clean them, you
care for orphans, you carry all the burdens of the family
in the besieged city. And your smile illuminates the whole
life of the city, like a ray of sunshine.
Alexander Fadeyev 1944

'This flat is falling to pieces,' I say. 'The toilet seat is cracked and the shower sprays all over the bathroom. A wall tile fell on my toe this morning.'

Lena whirls around the room, gathering papers and stuffing them into her briefcase. 'You don't need to tell me. I just haven't the time to do anything about it.'

'Surely that's the landlord's job?'

She pauses to stare at me.

'No, seriously.'

'Look.' She enunciates the word clearly, as though talking to an idiot. 'I once renovated a room myself. Wallpapered it, painted it. And what happened? The owner threw me out. Thanks to me, she could let it for a higher rent.'

'Isn't that against the law?'

Her laugh is bitter. 'I thought you'd lived in Russia. Anyway, I'm late already. Meet me later and we'll go for a walk.'

By six in the evening we are strolling along a promontory bordered by a narrow strip of sand. We are almost at the Neva's mouth. Couples push old-fashioned hooded prams beneath silver birch trees; teenagers congregate on benches drinking beer. Brown-limbed boys climb a concrete pill-box left over from wartime defences, *Danger – do not climb* painted on its side. They run along its roof and hurl themselves into the water, trying to make the biggest splash. A little girl in starched frills stands on the shore watching them.

'It is a sort of masochism to live in this city. Dostoevsky said you rarely find such a gloomy and strange climatic influence on the soul as here in Petersburg,' says Lena.

'I've seen worse places.'

'Oh this is just a happy interlude. It'll be snowing in two months' time.' She sighs. 'In winter you rarely see the sun. The wind comes straight off the Gulf. Walking into it makes you weep.'

We sit down on the hot sand and kick off our shoes, wriggling our toes into the coolness beneath the surface.

'But then,' she says, 'it's like being hopelessly in love. I can never give this city up.'

'Have you tried?'

'I found Moscow full of greed; the west even worse. People there live like hungry ghosts – never satisfied, always seeking more.'

Her attention reverts to the boys. She laughs with them.

'Lena.' I touch her arm. 'I've been meaning to ask you – why are people so eager to find me a husband?'

Her eyebrows lift. 'They want to help you.'

'Maybe I like living alone.'

'We don't.'

'You know I love Russia, Lena, but sometimes your sense of collectivism drives me crazy.'

'And your individualism is the hardest aspect of western life for me to accept,' she counters. 'Do you remember that I lived with a Pakistani family in London? I felt so much more at home among them than among you, although I am officially European. Their Asian way of life and values were what I knew; yours weren't.'

Centuries ago my forebears also lived in a world where there was little distinction between the individual and the community. Lena's not-so-distant heritage was the peasant *mir*, the commune. This word has two lovely synonyms: 'world' and 'peace'.

'And,' she adds, 'it saved us during the siege.'

'Undoubtedly. But this is peacetime. I don't see why it has to extend to another person's domestic arrangements.

She laughs. 'You're an individualist even among westerners.'

We walk on along the shore. A man obviously the worse for wear is being helped home by two women whom I take to be his wife and mother. The man protests weakly, 'Give a man a drop for pity's sake...'

The women, clutching his arms, make soothing sounds. We stand aside to make way for the trio as they pass.

'A familiar sight,' I say.

Lena shrugs.

I won't let the subject drop. 'I know that women run this country. I know they do all the housework and childcare. And the dirty, exhausting ill-paid jobs. Why are they so willing to accept any man who comes along? I see it all the time.'

Lena stops in her tracks. 'We lost 27 million in the war. Most of the dead were men. That left millions of 'surplus' women. And those were the women who brought up this generation.'

My cheeks burn. 'Sorry. I should have realised.' I remember a great-aunt telling me about the competition to 'catch' a man after the First World War.

'And in provincial Russia,' I say, 'I learned that a woman has to marry by twenty-five or she is on the shelf. I thought Petersburg might be different.'

'Why should it be? It bestows status to be married, you see. No matter who to. It's an old belief system.'

Ivan once tried to explain to me why he was not married at thirty-five. He said he only met women who were interested in his money. Perhaps that was true; perhaps his projection, but the question of age had never occurred to me, nor his bachelor status.

'But you're not married, Lena.'

'Not through choice.'

'I didn't realise…'

'I would have liked a child.'

'You don't need a husband for that.'

She rolls her eyes at me. 'I struggle to support myself, let alone a child.'

'Did you never meet anyone?'

'No one I could consider marrying.'

'What about Osman?'

She bursts out laughing.

'He's devoted.'

'I've given up,' she wipes her eyes. 'Our relationship went on for years. On and off. I ended it finally, last year.'

'Why?'

'Again, it was too hard. He was brought up by Naima and his grandmother. By women. Like many men of our generation. Actually he is a descendant of our nineteenth-century 'superfluous men' – those sensitive chaps beloved by our novelists. He's an eternal student. He writes exquisite poetry; he's never washed a pair of socks in his life. He lives off Naima of course.

'And the truth is,' her voice drops to a whisper, 'I don't have the experience myself.'

'Of a man?'

'A grown up man. There were never any in my life.'

Two men squat by the water's edge, their shirts laid out to dry on a rock. They take turns to shave each other's heads. Their necks are tattooed with angels. Not yet fashion accessories in Russia, tattoos are symbols of *blatnoi* – they tell prison stories. A matron in a flowered bathing hat waddles past the *zeks*. She plants her legs in the water and stands for a minute with hands on her hips. Then she lowers her rolls of flesh into the water and pushes off, pale limbs circling past us.

A sudden thought occurs to me. 'And what about your aunt?'

'She married a surgeon who survived the war. He was quite a bit older than her. They were sent out to work in the Nenets republic, not far from Novaya Zemlya where atomic testing was taking place. Her husband became ill but there was a lack of iodine to treat him. He died in 1974.'

The matron in the bathing hat has emerged from the

water and is striding towards us across the sand. She grips the arm of a small wet boy, as though she had just fished him up from the depths. He bites his lip and blinks hard.

She drags him past us and stops before a young woman sunbathing on a towel. 'Your boy jumped on top of me. You need to control him. Doesn't he have a father?'

The boy wriggles. 'Ma-aaa…'

'It happened with my own mother,' says Lena. 'She said she knew my father would leave – even before she married him. She just wanted a husband's name on her passport – for my sake, and then she was prepared to let him go.'

She sighs. 'It's probably too late for me now.'

20

Those who have written die, but what has been written
remains. To write about a circle is to break the circle. A
deed whichever way you look at it. In the abyss of lost
time, something found.
Lidiya Ginzburg, Blockade Diary

Lena calls me to the phone. Tatiana Nikolaevna's cheerful voice booms down the line, informing me that she has rounded up another of her former team mates. 'We were lucky,' she declares. 'Alexander Nikolaevich is off to a conference. He's very busy. I caught him just in time.'

We shall meet tomorrow morning at the Anichkov Palace.

'Come with me,' I invite Lena. 'Meet the Communists.'
She hesitates.

'Oh come on. Remember Professor Tikhvinskii; drop the prejudice for once.'

'All right. You win.'

Tatiana Nikolaevna bounds across the Palace forecourt with the vigour of a Young Pioneer. Despite herself, Lena smiles. A grey figure shuffles behind her. Tatiana waits for him to catch up.

'Alexander Rouptsov,' he wheezes as he bows to us. Despite the heat Rouptsev is elegantly dressed in a tailored suit.

Tatiana leads us up to the room in which we sat with Professor Tikhvinskii last week. Rouptsov takes a seat without fuss and folds his hands on the table.

Tatiana Nikolaevna nods at him. 'You may begin.'

He bows his head. 'Perhaps the siege is even more terrifying now when you look back.'

His voice has the low pitch and measured tempo of a man used to commanding attention. 'The soldier-poet Yulia Drudina wrote that she only once engaged in hand-to-hand fighting, but did so a thousand times in her sleep. Whoever says war isn't frightening, knows nothing at all about war.'

He leans back in his chair. 'But in those days you could not afford to dwell upon your fear.'

Across the table the aubergine head nods vigorously.

'It was dangerous. It could mean a death sentence. You had to play your part, to do what was necessary for victory.'

He is silent for so long that I wonder if he has fallen asleep.

'Alexander Nikolaevich,' Tatiana prompts in a gentle tone, 'why don't you tell us about yourself?'

He smoothes a paper in front of him, a certificate for harvesting potatoes in 1943. 'In the autumn of 1941 I joined a street lighting brigade. We took down the beautiful nineteenth-century iron lamps on Nevsky Prospect. We cleaned those lamps, wrapped them up for protection and stored them in cellars. It was so important for us children to feel a sense of participation, that we were contributing towards the war effort. Most important of all, looking after those lamps was an act of faith, a statement of belief in victory, an assertion that one day they would be restored to their rightful places.'

A bluebottle buzzes against the window pane. The room is stifling. My eyelids droop. I begin to feel a sense of disconnection, of floating above the city, away from its traffic and melting tarmac.

'To a large degree,' Rouptsev continues, 'I owe my survival, both physical and spiritual, to my teachers. They are people who departed this world a long time ago. My literature teacher, Alexandra Mikhailovna Filipchenko, instilled in me a love of the written word.'

He lifts his head; his cheeks are tinged with pink.

'Even "love" sounds banal when I consider all that literature means to me. Alexandra Mikhailovna taught me to see how literature penetrates the essence of our existence.'

Lena sits very still, her eyes fixed on Rouptsev's face.

'During the siege, as we began to starve, I listened to readings on the radio. Every day Olga Bergholtz performed *Readings to be Continued.*'

'Oh,' interjects Tatiana. 'Don't you remember *Red Sails?*'

'Alexander Grin.' Rouptsev smiles. 'You see, for us those readings created a bridge between one day and the next. They were nothing like the soap operas of today. You listened in the knowledge that not everyone would live to hear the next episode. The thought worked on one's subconscious: I too shall live – I shall be one of those who hears tomorrow's instalment.

'I read that Bergholtz herself fell in the snow one day,' says Lena. 'She was so weak. She heard her own voice coming from somewhere above her head and thought that it was an effect of being dead. The she realised it was a broadcast she had recorded some hours before and it was being relayed from a street receiver.'

'Oh the radio helped to save us,' continues Rouptsev. 'We should have died; our rations were too small to sustain human life.'

'Quite true,' agrees Tatiana.

'In physical terms, a person cannot survive on that minimum. It is impossible!' Rouptsev raises his voice, as though I might have difficulty believing him. 'Impossible!'

'But that spiritual element, that intangible, immeasurable force exemplified by those radio readings, was a vital supplement to our bread rations.'

Lena's eyes meet mine; my skin tautens.

Rouptsev smiles at us from across the table, lines scything upwards from the corners of his eyes. 'I once spent three years working in Cuba – I am a professor of law – and I remember the intense blue of the sea there, as though it were lit from within. Literature illuminates our lives like that, if you allow it.'

❧

Lena has organised a soirée. She spends the day shopping and preparing *zakuski,* a smorgasbord of salads and pots of mushrooms baked in cream. I try to help, washing and scraping vegetables.

'No, not like that. The mushrooms have to be chopped, not sliced.'

I lay down the knife and wipe my brow. 'Is it the siege or is it flu? I feel light-headed, feverish.'

'Everyone is out of sorts,' replies Lena. 'There's a magnetic storm.'

I gaze out of the window at a radiant sky.

'Where?'

'In the cosmos. Go and lie down. Our guests will be here at seven.'

She returns to rolling pastry.

At six Aunt Nadya leaves the flat. 'She does not care for of this sort of occasion,' says Lena.

I sit down on my sofa-bed and start reading the memoir of the opera singer Galina Vishnevskaya. Abandoned by her parents as a baby, she was brought up by her father's mother. They suffered the siege together until one evening her grandmother's dress caught alight as she sat by the *borzhoika* stove. She burned to death despite Vishnevskaya's attempts to save her.

Vishnevskaya almost gave up: *I grew steadily weaker. I spent all my time sleeping or daydreaming of beautiful, unobtainable things…*

In her dreamlike state she watched a detachment of women retrieve corpses from apartments, in order to dispose of them before epidemics broke out in the warmer weather. Finally three women came to her door and found her alive. She was taken to the local anti-aircraft defence HQ where she was fed and restored to life.

Towards the end of the siege, she described how *people literally rose from the dead to reach out for art*. She watched an opera company perform Tchaikovsky's *The Queen of Spades* with their breath steaming in the cold air. *The thrill I felt was not simply the pleasure of a great performance: it was pride in my resurrected people, in the great art which compelled those human shadows – the musicians, the singers, the audience – to come together in that opera house, beyond whose walls air raid sirens wailed and shells exploded…*

I am awakened by the door bell. Osman enters, kisses our hands, and produces a jar of apple juice. I ask him if it is difficult to be Muslim in this hard-drinking country.

He smiles. 'I am Sufi. Of course a Russian is suspicious of a non-drinker. He feels threatened. I don't go out much.'

A group of youngish men in black leather surge into the kitchen behind Osman. Artyum, Piotr and Vadim reach into their jackets and place bottles of beer and vodka on the table. I am introduced to a thin bespectacled man, Volodya. Long hair flops from a side parting, shielding a sallow face.

'Volodya is reading for us tonight,' says Lena.

'You are English?' Cold fingers grip my arm. 'Perhaps you would be so kind as to look at this. It is my poem. Part of it is in English. Tell me if there are any corrections needed.'

He thrusts a sheaf of papers onto the table in front of me and watches as I struggle to decipher the words. *The valley shade of the death…*

Volodya's eyes are on my face, waiting for a reaction. He scratches his elbows. Beads of sweat glisten on his temples.

'This is from the Bible?' I ask.

'Of course.'

'In the valley of the shadow of death…' I begin.

Volodya glares at me, gathers up his papers and goes over to seek admiration from a red-haired woman who has just arrived. She listens to him with the expression of blank stupor I have seen so often on the faces of Russian women in the presence of men – a mask that drops in their own company.

I try in vain to catch Osman's eye. He sits cross-legged on a cushion in the corner and stares at the wall. The men crack open more bottles.

'Caroline is researching the siege,' Lena announces.

All eyes turn towards me. 'But that is wonderful.' Volodya walks over to my side and puts a clammy hand on mine, all offence forgiven. 'It is a story about freedom.'

'I don't quite understand…'

'You must know that the *blokadniki* lost everything – almost. The one thing they did not lose was their freedom. The precious element that defines us as human beings.'

He jumps to his feet and looks around in agitation. 'Lenochka, Lenochka…' he whispers into her ear. She goes over to her bookshelves and takes down a slim volume. Volodya snatches it and riffles through the pages. 'Where is it… Ah, here!' He reads, *We who lived in concentration camps can remember the men who walked through the huts comforting others, giving away their last piece of bread. They may have been few in number, but they offer sufficient proof that everything can be taken from a man but one thing: the last of human freedoms – to choose one's attitude in any given set of circumstances, to choose one's own way.* Volodya looks around the assembled company with an air of defiance.

'What is the book?' I ask.

'Victor Frankl: *Man's Search for Meaning.*' Pinprick pupils bore into mine. 'Tolstoy put it another way, if you like. He said that people cannot be placed against their will in situations opposed to their conscience. No matter how terrible our circumstances we always have the opportunity to exercise our choice.'

'It is true,' the red-haired woman adds in a smoky drawl. 'We have the freedom to stop at any time and say, 'Enough! I will live differently from now on.'

'I had two great-uncles,' says Piotr. 'Both men of enormous wealth and culture. At the time of the revolution the Bolsheviks seized everything: houses, furniture, land, the lot. As "former people", they were allocated corners of rooms in communal flats. Of course they were forbidden to practise their professions. One uncle shot himself; the other went to work as a janitor at the Putilov works. He adapted. I remember him as a cheerful old man whose greatest pleasure was a spoonful of jam with his tea. This was a man who had danced with Grand Duchesses and conversed with Sigmund Freud.'

'It is interesting,' says Lena, 'that you cannot predict in advance how anyone will act. They say that during the siege refined members of the intelligentsia stole their children's rations, while people who in peacetime had been greedy and uncouth suddenly became the comforters, the ones who gave away their last piece of bread.'

'Precisely my point,' says Volodya. 'Our response to circumstance is not necessarily determined by circumstance. That is the essence of free will. Dostoevsky said he prayed to be worthy of his suffering.'

I am enjoying myself. I remember how Ivan had no time for the intelligentsia. Mostly too poor to be of use to him, they passed beneath his radar. Once we had gone to a party thrown by his former English teacher. Her husband, a professor, had got very drunk and lauched into a diatribe against the new businessmen, calling them parasites and scum. I was offended on Ivan's behalf. But afterwards he just laughed and said that the professor was afraid. People of his sort had been complacent for too long, their positions secure under the old system. Now they were being forced to confront the real world and it terrified them. You too, he had said. I asked him what he meant. For once he grew serious. He knew I didn't approve of his work, and of course it would be nice to read poetry all day long. I just had no idea how hard it was to live in Russia.

He had made his choice, and found his justifications.

Raised voices pull me from my thoughts. Volodya is shouting at Artyum. He goes to the bathroom, locks the door and remains for a long while.

'What was all that about?' I ask Lena.

'T. S. Eliot. Artyum said *The Wasteland* was a great poem. Volodya took offence.'

'Perhaps it's the magnetic storm.'

She sighs. 'Perhaps.'

Volodya flings open the bathroom door and staggers towards us. Osman gets up, takes his arm, walks him to the front door and helps him on with his shoes. Volodya is trying to argue but his words are slurred and indistinct. It seems to be a signal for the party to break up. Sombre faces file out after them, bidding us goodnight.

I help Lena to clear up the remains of the *zakuski*. She is quiet.

'I think Volodya is taking drugs,' I say. 'Perhaps heroin.'

She sighs. 'I've known him since our university days. He has been depressed for a while. But I had no idea…'

The phone rings. Lena answers it and then returns to the kitchen. 'That was Osman. You were right. He is trying to get Volodya into a clinic.'

'Doesn't it depend on Volodya?'

'What?'

'Well it's his choice. Otherwise it won't work.'

I hope he makes the right one.

Finally, when the flat is clean, we lean on the balcony rail together to watch the sun sink behind the blocks opposite.

Flopping down onto a stool, Lena looks drained. 'Tonight I almost feel nostalgic for Soviet days. It sounds crazy. We were persecuted, we had to watch ourselves all the time, but you can't imagine the solidarity we had. At times I felt intensely alive. You see, I get so tired of working with New Russians. They are not interested in studying. They bribe their way to degrees.'

I remember the girl who collided with me last week but keep my mouth shut.

'All day long I work among people with more ambition than culture. Tonight I suppose I wanted to recreate something from our past…'

'Did you ever get into trouble? In those days, I mean.'

'Not personally, but of course I knew people who did. One of my fellow students was sent to a mental hospital for practising yoga.'

She brushes back the hair from her face and grins. 'You see, the security organs were not noted for their subtlety. One day a couple of workmen came to our hostel and told us they were repairing the telephone in the hall. There was nothing wrong with it.'

'KGB?'

'Of course. We took care not to say anything important near the telephone. It wasn't just taps, they put microphones in them, to pick up voices in the vicinity.'

Once a colleague of Ivan's showed me his identity card. 'The most feared,' he had laughed. *Major X… Komitet Gosudarstvenii Bezopastnost*. I had been shocked. But of course the KGB and their successors make up many of the new business elite. They have the connections and the information. I never cared for that man. He always knocked too loudly when he visited, as though he wanted to break down the door.

❧

Lena greets me with a kiss on the cheek.

'You look happier,' I say.

'I finished Boldyrev's *Siege Notes*.' She pulls the book from her bag and lays it on her desk. 'I've been so busy

I haven't had time until today. But Lord, did it make me hungry. I went through borscht, blinis, potatoes and cutlets – everything on the canteen menu.'

She places the book in my hands and fills the samovar. 'Here, read this entry.'

Boldyrev describes an elderly bachelor, an aesthete and ballet lover who refuses to leave Leningrad. He is on the lowest rations, so weak his legs can barely carry him. He creeps along the street, too slow to catch his tram, and yet he persists in spending a large part of his salary on books.

Over my shoulder Lena reads aloud, '*Such courage, such strong-willed resolution to overcome the law that says 'to eat is to live.' A powerful rebellion against the animalistic yoke. At the beginning of our conversation he announced his aversion to the subject of food and rations. Now there's a man!*'

Eyes shining, her cheeks flushed, Lena squeezes my hand. 'There you are! That man was able to transcend siege conditions.'

'Did he survive?'

She shrugs. 'Physically you mean? Boldyrev doesn't say. But that's not the point.'

'What about Boldyrev himself?'

'You mean what pulled him through? Precisely this.' She taps the book. 'As the siege wore on he began to realise the significance of his diary. It was more important to him than all his other work. He wrote that it would be more than a miserable record of food consumed, more than a death rattle, it would be a truthful witness to the time.

'Let me show you, I marked the page.'

And there arises in my mind's eye an undreamed-of pleasure: a study, warm and light. Alive, well-fed, clean and calm, I sit and write. All horrors are in the past. 'Siege

Notes' – are notes about the past and in the past. The diary is finished and I am preparing it for others to read.

'He wrote that on 15 December 1942,' Lena continues. 'The second winter of the siege. He had another year to go, but already his spirit was vaulting over the horrors.'

21

In the Pushkin Theatre auditorium the tempera-
ture was three degrees below zero. The public, the
defenders of Leningrad, sat in their overcoats and
I was playing in gloves with the fingers cut off.
But how they listened and how I played!... as soon
as I realised why I was playing, I felt what and
how I must play, so that some works which used
to be my favourites had all of a sudden become
meaningless... Perhaps it was then that I first
understood and sensed in my bones the greatness
of Beethoven's Appasionata...
Vladimir Sofronitsky – *The Duty of an Artist*

The young man's foot shoots into the gap between the
lift doors. He wrenches them apart with tattooed hands.

'Please.' His smile illumines the gloom.

I glance at the scorch marks blackening the lift
buttons.

'Thanks, I'll walk up.'

There are eight floors to climb. On the fifth landing I sidestep a pile of shit. Catching my breath as I

reach the top, I press a buzzer set in a padded door. The composer Zhanna Metallide stands before me, a sturdy figure in shirt and trousers. She ushers me into a sunny room full of books. A piano stands against the wall by a window that gives a panoramic view over the chimneys and factories of the Vyborg Side.

'I am sorry I can't make tea. The water is off again.' She shrugs off my expression of sympathy. 'What can you do? This is the eighth floor. At this level the pressure is very low.'

She offers me cake and a fizzy orange drink.

'My music is inspired by Russian folk tales and the places I have visited. I have travelled all around the Soviet Union. Last year I composed an opera based on the legends of the Siberian Hantsi-Mantsi people.'

On the wall is a photograph of Zhanna in waders, fishing rod in hand, beaming at the camera.

She places a booklet in my hands. 'About my life as a composer.'

'I believe you lived through the siege.'

A pause. 'Yes. My classmates were evacuated when war broke out but my parents stayed behind. My father had lost some toes in the Finnish war – frostbite – so he could not go to the front. In 1942 he was arrested…'

Another disappearance, another silence.

'But it is not important.' Zhanna's voice brisk. 'Let us return to music.

'We lived in a huge communal flat. One of our neighbours was a professional pianist. She inspired me. I picked up music by ear. I sang. I danced. I had boundless creative energy. During the siege we kids gave concerts at a hospital on Nevsky Prospect. I played accompaniment. After the war I entered the composers' faculty at the Conservatoire.'

I am at a loss. We are not touching the subject. Perhaps

I have not found the right questions. I search for words, but of course these are not her language. If I had a better understanding of hers I could read her scores, listen to recordings. The piano stands mute in the corner.

'Excuse me for a moment.' She rises to her feet. 'I have to speak to my daughter.' She leaves the room. The booklet is still in my hands. I flip through its pages. *In 1942 Lazar Metallide was shot for 'counterrevolutionary economic activities'... My mother's life was destroyed... she grew hardened, embittered. Life was not easy for my brother Petya and me.*

The eight-year-old Zhanna had to support her mother, her baby brother and herself by selling family possessions on the streets.

And then a question arises. Zhanna lost her father; so did Valentina Pavlovna, Nonna Borisovna... and what of Lena's forebears? She never speaks of them. All I know is that her grandfather died before the war. The family were intellectuals and native to Leningrad. Perhaps they were Communists, perhaps not. It made little difference to a person's fate. I wonder at my own obtuseness.

Zhanna returns.

'You had an extremely hard time during the siege.'

Dark eyes gleam behind heavy spectacles. 'All that hardship taught me to value life. Others became disheartened and sank into darkness, but not I. When you walk on the razor's edge you value life all the more. At least, that is true for me.'

It is another hot evening. The packed bus crawls towards the Finland Station along the Valley of Death, as this stretch of road was once called. Evacuation transports left from the station. Knowing this, the Germans shelled its approaches.

A girl slumps in the aisle, her face ashen. A couple of women stand up and press her into the seat they have vacated. She mumbles something and they help her off at the next stop, watching as she staggers and almost falls. 'Probably a drug addict…'

Should I get off and try to help her? But what could I do? And if I miss this bus I'll never get on another at this hour… The doors slam shut and the vehicle pulls away from the kerb. The girl is leaning against a kiosk, her eyes shut. Perhaps some passer-by will recognise her and help her home.

I scare myself. How easy it is to look the other way.

❦

As I reach our courtyard I remember that it is Saturday, the day when Pavel plays his outdoor concert. But there is only Sveta, sitting alone on the bench, head bent. She doesn't see me approach. I sit down beside her. With a start she raises her head. Black eyeliner maps out crows feet; pink rivulets stain her upper lip.

'What happened? Where is Pavel?'

'He can't play today. Last week we had some bad news. The day after you came to tea. His son was murdered.'

'Your son?'

She shakes her head. 'His. By his first marriage. Kostya got involved with some businessmen. Mafia. He owed money. They stabbed him in a lift.'

A tear slides down her apple cheek. 'So you see, that is why Pavel couldn't play for you last week. I wanted to apologise. I was cross with him, but he is very sensitive. We hadn't heard the news yet but his heart must have known.'

When I reach the flat I run into the bathroom and splash my face with water. Flipping down the toilet lid, I sit down, shaking. I am desperately sorry for the accordionist; I am also undergoing a delayed reaction to events that took place years ago. One day my neighbour, a retired factory worker came running into my room in alarm. She had found Ivan at the entrance to the flats, bleeding and barely conscious. She had called an ambulance. He was attacked in the street, she said. A carload of men had sat waiting for him. A passer-by, who happened to be a boxer, had seen what was going on and chased his attackers off, but Ivan was left with a broken rib and concussion. I visited him in hospital, bringing him a bowl and cutlery so that he could eat. It was a public hospital – if you didn't have utensils you went hungry.

It had been a warning. In response Ivan told me to get a message to a retired army colonel he knew. 'What about the police?' I asked.

'You don't understand Russia. The police are not interested. Go to Colonel G…'

The Colonel was a charming man for whom I had once brought a Savile Row shirt at Ivan's request. When I told him that Ivan was in hospital he looked grave. Sudden fear shot through me. 'They must know about me, too.'

The colonel flicked his hand. 'They won't touch you. We'll sort out those riff-raff.'

Everyone in business had to have a *krisha*, or protector. The Colonel's men paid a visit to Ivan's assailants, who took off back to the small town whence they had come. 'Hoping to move onto my patch,' said Ivan. 'Scum like that try it all the time. They think they have nothing to lose. But they forgot to sort out their own protection first. Idiots.' He laughed.

I woke up then.

When he came out of hospital Ivan took me to view the flat by the Volga, and I knew it was time to leave.

Lena comes home late that evening. I tell her about Pavel's son.

'A dreadful and all too common story these days. I'll light a candle for the poor young man. So many of them fall prey to temptation. It's all new you see, they make material goods their holy grail…'

22

The most terrible road of all!
At the twentieth verst – how could I go on?
Hundreds of children from the city
coming towards me…
Hundreds of children!
Freezing along the way…
Children by themselves
On ice torn up by bombs;
They could not recognise death
When it dived down upon them
Their uncomprehending eyes.
Followed a shooting star
Alexander Mezhirov

'What is your name and where do you come from?' The concierge is interested, not officious.

I tell her.

'And my name is Emilia. Pleased to meet you. Elena Vyacheslavovna is detained for a few minutes. She asks you to wait.'

Emilia indicates a row of red plush flip seats along the wall. I sit down.

'How do you like our city?' she asks.

'It's beautiful.'

Emilia looks as though she should have retired years ago.

'May I ask, did you live through the siege?' I have grown bolder.

Her hesitation is momentary. 'I did. I was five when it began. My sister was three. We lost our mother. She gave me her last drop of medicine and then she died.'

'How did you survive?'

'Our aunt took us in. She was eighteen. She worked in a canteen and she was able to bring a little soup home for us. I learned to dance at the Palace of Pioneers. After I got married my husband and I danced with Igor Moiseyev. That was in the nineteen fifties.'

'Oh, he's world famous. You must have been wonderful dancers.'

'We did our best.' Her lips tighten. 'But life is hard for us today. We lived better in Stalin's time.'

A door opens behind Emilia and a man in overalls emerges. 'My husband Kiril.' Emilia brightens. 'We have been invited to a wedding but have nothing to take. We have been arguing about it.'

'It's too expensive,' says Kiril. 'Better not to go.'

'I was talking to this English lady about the siege.'

He reads the question in my eyes. 'I was evacuated,' he says. 'I was ten years old. They sent us across Lake Ladoga and then in freight-wagons to Siberia where they put us in orphanages. I lost my sister somewhere near Novosibirsk.' He opens his mouth and howls, 'Oh why remember that time? It was so hard to bear.'

Larisa remembered nothing of her evacuation from Leningrad, except that on the far shore of Lake Ladoga she was put on a train and sent to Kuibyshev, as Samara was called in Soviet days. She was sent to a children's home where she grew up.

Stricken, I stare at the lone gold tooth which stands like a tombstone in Kiril's lower gum and search for inspiration. 'Which football team do you support?'

'Zenit.'

A local team. 'Didn't they win the cup in 1944?'

'That's right! Just after the siege was lifted.' Kiril brightens. 'The team was officially evacuated to Kazan but some players remained in Leningrad. They held matches during the siege... Some died of starvation; some died at the front, but we still beat both Spartak and Dynamo in that year.' His eyes shine. 'And how are our Russian players doing in your English league?'

The clack of heels on parquet. Lena appears, followed by a fat man in a suit. She nods a curt dismissal to him and he leaves the building without acknowledging us.

This is the first time I have seen Lena in her work environment. She radiates authority, a younger model of her aunt.

'Lena, I was just talking to Kiril and Emilia about the siege.'

She bestows a vague smile upon the couple.

'It was good to recall that time after all,' Kiril thanks me. 'Here's our address. Come and pay us a visit.'

We emerge from the lobby onto the Griboyedov Canal. On the opposite bank stands the Church of the Spilled Blood, erected on the spot where Tsar Alexander II was blown up by a terrorist bomb in 1881. The cathedral domes are twists of turquoise, green and gold, modelled on St Basil's in Moscow's Red Square. Their reflections shimmer like spinning tops in the still waters of the canal. Turning right, we walk towards Nevsky Prospect. I stop in front of a bakery with a large white cake in the window, looped with iced garlands and studded with pink roses.

'Wait,' I tell Lena. I enter the baker's, buy the cake in the window, and carry it back down the canal to the office building. I plant the box on Emilia's lap. 'For you. Enjoy the wedding.' She throws up her hands. I hurry away before she can speak.

Lena and I take a detour home through streets warmed by evening rays, leaving behind the commercialism of Nevsky. It is easy in Petersburg to feel close to its past. Following the Griboyedov Canal, we skirt around Peter the Great's mysterious New Holland wharves, long abandoned but well preserved, as though it were only yesterday that his ships unfurled their sails and slipped away. We emerge onto the English Embankment. A flight of steps leads to the Neva. We sit, lulled by the lap of wavelets on granite. The sky glows gold. Distant cranes drop their arms over the city as if in benediction. The wind across the water carries with it a scent of something old and wholly familiar.

'Port cities have this scent,' I say. 'London, Liverpool, New York, Shanghai... It's quite distinctive – the smell of expansion...'

Arms clasped around her knees, Lena gazes across the river towards the docks. 'Peter the Great must have caught it three hundred years ago.'

I seize the moment. 'Lena?'

'Mmm?'

'What happened to your grandfather?'

Her face darkens. 'I don't know anything about my father's side. He left us when I was small. Remarried.'

'I meant your maternal grandfather.'

'He was shot during the purges.'

Two sphinxes on the Robespierre Embankment have half woman/half skull faces and gravity-defying bosoms – a post-Soviet style of sculpture that eschews subtlety for impact. Bronze plaques on their plinths are engraved with excerpts from poems: Akhmatova's *Requiem*, Mandelstam, Brodsky…

'*To the victims of political repression,*' I read.

Standing between the sphinxes, we peer through a grilled aperture at the Kresty (Crosses) prison on the other side of the Neva. It is built in the Strangeways school of penal architecture.

'Kresty was founded by Peter the Great's niece, the Empress Anna Ivanovna and extended in the nineteenth-century,' says Lena, who has walked me up here beneath a crimson evening sky.

'I want to pinch myself.' I link my arm through hers. 'You and I grew up during the Cold War – for me that was an eternal state of affairs that would outlast my lifetime… and yet here we are.'

Lena shakes her head. 'Don't be fooled. This is not the 1930s, nor even the 1970s but it still goes on. Last November my aunt and I, and thousands of others, paid our last respects to Galina Starovoitova.'

Starovoitova was the leader of the Democratic Russia party and a human rights activist who negotiated to prevent the first war with Chechnya. When talks failed she called Yeltsin 'Boris the Bloody'. She was gunned down on the stairs of her apartment building by the Griboyedov Canal.

'We queued for hours, in freezing temperatures. She was uncorrupted. Perhaps our last democrat.'

'Did they catch her killers?'

'Of course not.* It was a warning. There will be more Starovoitovas. Things don't change so quickly around here.'

Lena recites from *Requiem:*

'…If someday in this country

They decide to raise a memorial to me,
I will consent to this honour
On one condition only – do not build it
By the sea where I was born,
I have severed my last ties with the sea;
Nor in the Tsar's garden by the sacred stump
Where an inconsolable shadow seeks me;
But here where I stood for three hundred hours
And no one opened the bars to me.
For even in blessed death I fear
That I will forget the Black Marias,
Forget the malice of the doors' slam

And the old woman's howl, like a wounded beast.
Let the melting snow stream like tears
From my motionless bronze lids
And let the prison dove coo in the distance
While ships sail calmly down the Neva.

'Akhmatova is our city,' Lena explains. 'A "gay little sinner" who underwent a transformation when the "true twentieth century" began with the outbreak of war in 1914. From then onwards, until her death in 1966, she survived war, revolution and Chekist terror – her former husband Nikolai Gumilev was shot in 1922. During

---

* In 2005 two men were sentenced for Starovoitova's killing. It is still unclear who ordered her assassination.

the purges of the 1930s she was virtually silenced, then she lived through the early days of the siege, then she was silenced again under the "Zhdanovschina", when Andrei Zhdanov denounced her as "half-nun, half-whore."' Zhdanov was Chairman of the Soviet Union and director of cultural policy.

'Yet she wrote all the same.'

'She could not do otherwise. And then she burned her work. She had one of her friends commit each line to memory. *Requiem* survived in the mind of Lidiya Chukovskaya. Akhmatova would look up at the ceiling of her apartment – where she assumed microphones were hidden – and say something as innocent as "Would you like a cup of tea?" Then she would scribble down some lines. Chukovskaya memorised them and afterwards Akhmatova burned the paper in an ashtray.'

Akhmatova's friend, the poet Osip Mandelstam, wrote, *Only in Russia is poetry respected; it gets people killed.* Mandelstam died in a transit prison during the purges.

Anna Alexeeva too, was aware of the dangers. Just after the revolution she studied poetry under Nikolai Gumilev. In the 1930s the head of Leningrad's Poetry Academy advised her to stick to prose.

Anna Alexeeva ignored his advice.

On the tram home I take her book from my bag and read an excerpt from one of her letters:

... I have diagnosed myself: I am suffering from soul sickness, and they have not yet learned how to treat the soul. People such as I are usually sent to a psychiatric hospital, but there they treat only our physical brains. The brain and the soul are two different things. You can treat the brain, but the soul is elusive. What sort of medicine could cure her?

... This is all my fault. I have neglected my career. I devote all my free time to writing poetry... As long as you are

unknown you can live a peaceful life. As soon as you start to be published, look out. Someone takes exception to your lines, they misinterpret them, distort them, they find a hidden meaning and then goodbye quiet life and everything else.

'Do you think,' I ask Lena, 'that perhaps, in a horrible way, the purges prepared people to some degree?'

'For the siege?'

'They had already undergone enormous hardships. For years they had been living under the threat of the early morning knock at the door. What's more, anyone over thirty would have survived the revolution and civil war with all their terror and deprivation.'

'But they didn't know starvation. Not in Leningrad. During the early 1920s and 1930s it was the peasants who starved to death. In their millions. On the Volga, in Ukraine and southern Russia.'

'No, they had not faced starvation, but they had already cultivated an enormous degree of resilience.'

For despite the fear and the madness women and men went on writing. Reading a poem to a friend in secret, to ensure its survival, was as much an act of faith as taking down the street lamps and storing them away for some future day when peace and calm would return to the city.

23

We veterans don't choose our dreams,
They choose us
We still dream of war
As though the big guns keep us in their sights
We are shoved onto trains
Destination unknown
The blind dream of fire
The sated of bread rations
And those from whom we do not expect to hear
Come to visit us
Wartime friends drop by
Unaware that they no longer exist on this earth
Chance saved us from a shell
Whose fragments pierce our dreams
Stunned, we lie in darkness
On the no man's land between dream and reality
Vadim Shefner (recited by Ivan Dmitriev)

'Caroline!' People's Artist Ivan Petrovich Dmitriev stands in the doorway of his flat, arms outstretched. 'Thank you for coming.'

I step forward as though I were his long-lost leading lady and place my hands in his upturned palms. He leads me into a room filled with the subaqueous glow of sunlight filtering through a tangle of yucca and sweetheart leaves. 'All we have are books and plants – the most important things.' We cross to an open window and inhale the faint breath of the sea. 'When we first moved here we could see the Gulf of Finland,' he says. 'But they built these new apartment blocks which obscure the view.'

Photographs of Dmitriev in various roles hang on the walls. He opens a glass cabinet and pulls out a silver medal on a ribbon. 'Chairman Mao awarded me this when we filmed *Wind from the West* in China.'

A pale woman wheels in a trolley of tea and cakes. 'My wife, Galina Grigorievna.'

Galina has not been well. She listens while her husband talks. He relates the story of his young life in the provinces, how he joined a circus and came to Leningrad. He studied drama and then joined the Theatre of the Baltic Fleet. 'It employed the very best actors. They staged Molière, Gorky, Shakespeare…'

War broke out and he became trapped on the Hanko peninsula, four hundred kilometres from the city.

'I was with a brigade of twelve actors and musicians playing to the 26,000 sailors who had been guarding the straits. Our navy failed to prevent the enemy from encircling Leningrad. We were cut off for five months; the waters around us were mined.

'This posed a very specific problem for me as an actor – how to perform in front of those sailors? You know they are all thinking one thing: what's happening at home? To our families? No news came through to Hanko. So we could not entertain the troops as though nothing had happened, yet at the same time we had to try to stir those men. They were tired of the usual appeals: For Stalin! For the Motherland! People were criticising Stalin for having left us unprepared for war. They were losing faith.

'So I adopted a new mode of acting. I stood before those sailors in my own shock and grief. I spoke slowly, tears in my eyes, words catching in my throat. "Lads! What is your Motherland? What does it mean to you? Think about it for yourselves – the little garden you played in as a child with your brothers and sisters, all those who went before you and who now lie in its earth… This is what you have to defend."

'As I spoke two of our troupe would start to sing Russian folk songs, softly at first and then with full voice. Those sailors' eyes filled with tears.'

Dmitriev pauses to wipe his own eyes. 'When I perform I try to speak directly to the souls of my audience. And my soul responds to theirs. Let me tell you about one instance which happened at the front – later, after I had returned to the city. It was New Year's Eve and an officer called me over. He told me they were having trouble with a sniper who was insulting officers and picking fights with his comrades. I said I would see what I could do. They sent me to a dugout very near the enemy's positions. As I walked I could hear German voices floating down from the Peterhof Palace above us.

'I entered the trench. It was tiny, with room for only two people to sit, our knees touching. Before me I saw a man on the edge of despair.

'His name was Alexandrov and he was a crack sniper. He had learned that his wife and children had been killed. He sat hunched over, his black brows knitted together. "Who are you?" he growled.

'"I am an actor," I replied.

'"An actor? What on earth are you doing here?"

"An actor from the miniature theatre of trenches and dugouts. Would you like to hear a little Pushkin?"

'I began to recite. As I spoke I felt Alexandrov's attention deepen. Then I told a few jokes about Hitler. When I finished he brought his hands together, reluctantly at first, as though forcing himself. I lit a match and saw that something inside him had broken. Tears stood in his eyes.'

Dmitriev's eyes glisten. 'What is the soul? For me it is an invisible, living thing, closely connected to the emotions. It is what you feel stirring within you when you read Pushkin.'

'I hate war,' he says. 'It damns people. Now, at the end of our century in which so many millions have died, people are yet again killing their fellow human beings. I look at your Prime Minister, that young, smiling man, who is sending planes to drop bombs on living human beings in Kosovo.* Well that man is already dead in my eyes.'

'Were you a member of the Party?' I am suddenly curious.

'I was.' He reflects. 'You know, I used to believe in the collective life; I thought it was a splendid thing.'

He sets down his cup and frowns. 'But I saw the reality behind the propaganda. I would sit at banquets, listen to Party officials give speeches about the People, how the Party was the People, how it understood them, brought culture to them. Later, privately, I would hear them refer to the audience as rabble.'

His voice is heavy with sadness. 'In the collective you are responsible to nothing and to no one. A person loses

---

* He is referring to Tony Blair who was Prime Minister at the time.

his sense of values. He neither cultivates them in himself nor within society.'

'But you had a collective awareness during the siege.'

'Ah.' His face brightens. 'But that was on a different level – it was a choice we made, each of us as individuals. It was not imposed from above. Let me give you an example.' He straightens his right leg and rubs the knee. 'Old bones. That's better. Yes, well, I had a daughter, Natasha, who was killed in a bombing raid. We buried her at Serafimovskoye cemetery. On the way back I came across a little boy abandoned in the street. He was about two years old, filthy, dressed in an adult's quilted jacket.'

Dmitriev takes a slice of cake from the tea trolley. 'I decided to adopt that boy, but I was faced with the problem of how to feed him. My ration was not enough for two, even for a child. So I introduced him to my comrades. Each one of them donated five grammes from their fifty gramme sugar ration.'

'That was generous.'

'It was an act of great courage on their part. When you are starving five grammes seems an enormous amount to give away. But in fact it was the people who gave to others who survived. The person who withdrew into himself, who ate his ration all at once under his blankets – and I saw this happen – usually died.'

Dmitriev lifts his glass of tea to his lips. The liquid trembles. A drop trickles down his chin and falls, splodging his blue shirt.

'What happened to the boy?' I ask.

'He survived. He grew up, went to Tashkent. He drank... Well, it doesn't matter...' Dmitriev clears his throat. 'What else can I tell you? I haven't said much, it seems.'

'On the contrary.'

Galina Grigorievna pours out fresh tea. Her picture

hangs on the wall by the door, a pretty, heart-shaped face framed by a fur-trimmed cap.

'I was Gerda in the *Snow Queen.*'

I walk over to look at the photograph more closely. 'You remind me of Vivienne Leigh.'

'Oh thank you! She was my favourite.'

Using the arms of his chair as levers, Dmitriev pushes himself to his feet. Galina hands him two walking sticks that had been hooked over the arm of his chair. I hadn't noticed them until now. Only as he walks me to the door do I recall that he is eighty-five years old.

A fresh breeze wraps itself around me as I leave the Dmitrievs' flat. The sun is still high. I walk along the Embankment and then plunge into the 'Lines' of Vasilievsky Island – as its narrow, parallel streets are called. In this brilliant sunlight they remind me of the old fishing quarters of southern European ports, Cadiz perhaps, or Naples. Residents have spilled out of their overcrowded flats. Children play hopscotch on the pavement, *babushki* gossip on a bench and a young man leans against his doorway to admire passing girls.

When my legs tire I catch an almost-empty tram back to Lena's flat.

❧

Aunt Nadya is in the bathroom, feeding bed-linen into a machine balanced on a board stretched across the bathtub. I hover in the hallway. 'Can I help?'

She flicks a damp lock of hair from her forehead. 'I doubt it.'

Being realistic, so do I. From my experience in

Samara I know that there are some household tasks that neither foreigners nor men can be trusted to perform.

'While I keep an eye on this temperamental machine,' she says, as it rattles and spins, 'you can tell me who you saw today.'

'Ivan Dmitriev.' I raise my voice above the gurgle of waste water.

Aunt Nadya straightens, her stern jaw relaxing into a smile. 'How is he? I haven't seen him in years. He was well known after the war for always appearing dressed in a *tel'nyashka* – a striped sailor's shirt. And he had astonishing blue eyes.'

'He still has. He gave an extraordinary performance.'

'Here, hang these on the balcony.' She holds out a basin full of wet *Minzdrav* sheets. My arms sag with the weight. 'Oh damn this machine.' The tub is churning wildly now; a froth of soap suds spills to the floor. Before I can react Aunt Nadya seizes a cloth and goes down on her knees to mop the overflow.

I recall the anger I felt in Samara as I watched my neighbours boil up their washing water in heavy vats on the stoves in the *komunalka*. If this country can put people into space, I had thought, why can't it produce washing machines, even communal ones for each block of flats?

'Proper machines are expensive.' Aunt Nadya guesses my thoughts. 'And we would need a larger cable. That requires permission which means bribing a lot of people. The thought of it makes my head ache. Besides, it's not so bad compared to washing clothes in the freezing Neva.' She wrings out the floor cloth, grips the edge of the bath tub and pulls herself to her feet.

24

*All told, I am amazed at both the
cruelty of life and the wisdom with
which it balances our experiences of
hurt and rejection with love.*
Tamara Petkevich

'You've seen the violinist in our subway?' Lena dumps
the shopping on the kitchen table and flops onto a
stool. Vegetables roll from the collapsed bag.

'You mean the old woman with swollen legs?' I field
a garlic bulb as it falls to the floor.

'I spoke to her yesterday. She was a *zek*, a political
prisoner, arrested in the 1950s and sent to the Gulag.
After Stalin's death she was released and rehabilitated.'

The garlic is pink and moist in my hand. 'Marinated,'
says Lena.

I break off a clove and peel away the skin. 'That
woman plays very well.'

'The subway is the only stage she has. The Gulag
ended her musical career. Now she gets a pension of
eighty-three roubles and forty kopecks a month.'

The equivalent of two dollars.

'She has not worked the required number of years for a full pension.'

'She worked in the labour camp.'

'Doesn't count.' Lena pours herself a cup of tea. 'Talking of the Gulag, Aunt Nadya wants you to meet someone else. She didn't directly live through the siege, but her experience parallelled it.'

❧

I open the door of a pre-revolution block off Nevsky and pass through an entrance hall as cool and silent as a cathedral, its thick walls and doors shutting out the blazing street. Tamara Vladislavovna Petkevich looks younger than her eighty years but beneath carefully arranged hair her face is pale and exhausted. She ushers me into a book-lined room. 'Take a seat. I'll bring some water.'

She returns and sits down in a chair facing mine. 'This heat is extraordinary. It reminds me of Central Asia – I was exiled there before the war.'

'But you were born here?'

Tamara nods. 'I was born and brought up in Leningrad but I went to live in Tashkent in 1939. My husband had been sent into exile there and I accompanied him. In 1943 I was arrested and sent to a northern labour camp.

'My family stayed behind in Leningrad. My mother and youngest sister died in the siege. My father had been shot in the purges.'

The by-now familiar story.

She hands me a hardback book. 'My autobiography.' I study photos of Tamara's younger self. A stage portrait taken after she had been released from camp is almost too painful to behold. The pencilled arcs of her eyebrows, thick eyeliner and lipstick accentuate the agony they are designed to conceal.

'How long did you stay in the camps?'

'Seven years. I was in Belovodsk in the Komi region. For the first three and a half years I worked felling trees and quarrying rocks – the hardest physical labour.'

'Had you acted before?'

A smile of sudden sweetness illuminates her tired features. 'No. I was forced to become an actress. It was an order. Someone in the camp administration had seen a photo and sent for me.'

'But you had no experience.'

'My brigade helped me. Do you know what that word means?'

'Brigade? I think so.'

'In the camps your life depended on your work brigade. When you are quarrying stone you have to earn your ration or you die. How much bread you were given depended on how well you worked. Your brigade, your team, helped you to achieve your norm. You depend on each other. And so we had our theatre brigades of directors, performers and other professionals. I worked with interesting, talented people. They taught me how to act. They saved me.

'We played on makeshift stages set up in canteens. When the players entered in their costumes the audience were reminded that dresses existed. That in itself was a blessing.'

I picture a hall of rough-hewn wood, surrounded by barbed wire and pine forest so dense that light barely penetrates its canopy.

'During one of my first appearances I read out a story called "Wife" – a personal and honest account of the war experience. The female criminals who had beaten me up with sticks a few weeks beforehand wept.

'We travelled all around the Komi Republic to colonies far from any railway line. You can't imagine how wild that place was. Prisoners would return from work hungry and cold, wanting only to fall asleep on their bunks before they rose again at five in the morning. Nevertheless, when we arrived in the camp they would all come to see us. As soon as the music began they would start to cry, thinking of loved ones, of those far away.'

'Did they not envy you?'

'On one level, of course. Without a doubt our lives were incomparably better than theirs. We always felt guilty when we arrived at a camp and saw those sick, suffering beings. But we saw how we revived them too; we felt their gratitude.'

And how did those prisoners feel, I wonder, when the curtain fell? The Musical Comedy audience too, after the music had faded and the lights gone out? They emerged hungry into streets full of mortal danger.

Tamara sighs. 'I knew how they felt. When I was working in the logging camp a theatre troupe arrived one day. I can't remember much of the performance because I wept right through to the end. By that point I had come to accept the camp as a normal way of life. You never got used to it but you accepted it, you learned patience.'

'How?' The word bursts out too forcefully. My chest is tight; my throat burns. I am sad for this woman. Angry too, at the cruelty and waste.

'Because to imagine something beyond, to fantasise, involved physical and mental strength, and you didn't have any to spare.'

Tamara leans towards me, her eyes wide. 'Perhaps you have to suffer a great deal in order to understand the effect of creative expression on the spirit. Only then do you truly appreciate how it enables you to survive an ordeal. The human psyche is capable of enormous transformation. It is only by living through this process that you appreciate it.

'A person's talent is his breath of life.' As her voice quickens a faint flush comes to her cheeks. 'It needs expression, a creative outlet. If a prisoner could take that creative spirit out to even a tiny auditorium then he had a chance of survival in the camps. He was replenished. Without that opportunity death was almost certain.'

She leans back in her chair and puts her hand to her forehead as though the effort of speaking had exhausted her.

'Most prisoners were not so lucky of course. They were simply forced to mine, to quarry or fell trees. Thousands, millions of lives were wasted.'

'When were you released?'

'In 1950. As part of my sentence I was excluded from Leningrad. I couldn't live here but I used to travel in for the day. I wanted to learn of the circumstances in which my family had died. I had seen books and films about the siege and spoken to people who had lived through it. But the most powerful impression of all was made by an exhibition of paintings by siege survivors.' She begins to cry. 'They were amateurs, incapable of concealing their emotions beneath professional technique. Those pictures were so vivid, so fresh and immediate... they have scarred me for my whole life. I saw how my family died.'

I can't remember how I reach Lena's flat that evening.

❧

'So what was she like?' asks Lena over supper.

I try to describe Tamara but her image floats off beyond reach.

'It's strange. Unlike Dmitriev or Nonna Borisovna, she gave no performance. She was humble, down to earth.'

'An invaluable quality for an actress,' remarks Aunt Nadya.

Lena peers into my face. 'You look different. Brighter.'

'She revived me. Like those poor prisoners.'

'Her book is extraordinary,' says Aunt Nadya. 'She tells her story simply and without self-pity.'

She picks up my copy of Tamara's autobiography and flips through the pages.* 'It sold very well. In our country her experience was not so exceptional. It is our history. People could identify with her easily and ask themselves, "What would I have done if…?"'

'I wondered whether acting in the camps wasn't unintentionally cruel,' I say. 'Reviving people's memories like that. I was thinking about how the actors would vanish after the curtain fell, leaving the prisoners with nothing but their pain and hunger.'

Aunt Nadya slaps her hand on the table so hard that I jump. 'No!' she shouts. 'A thousand times no! The theatre brought people back from the dead, just as a person who stops breathing is given oxygen. You see', she grips my arm and stares into my eyes, 'it was so hard sometimes. Day after day you struggled to keep your spirits up. When you saw those crazy starving people

---

*   T. V. Petkevich, *Zhizn – Sapozhok Neparny* (Life is an Odd Shoe, Astra-Lux, St Petersburg, 1998)

on the streets it was like looking into a mirror. You were desperate not to cross that line, yet there were moments when you felt it might be easier to let go and to hell with it...' Her fingers fumble for her cigarette packet. 'On some days it was impossible to get up in the morning. You lay there feeling your life ebb away... Why even bother to get out of bed when your numb and swollen fingers would take ten minutes just to button your coat?

'But once,' she pauses to light a cigarette, 'in the darkest days of that first winter a friend came to see me. "I have two tickets for the Musical Comedy," he said. Those tickets were like gold dust. "Go away," I told him. I was lying in bed too weak to move. "You talk about the theatre when everyone is dying. They say on the radio that 20,000 starved to death yesterday."'

'My friend did not reply. Instead he went over to the closet and pulled out a dress. I'm ashamed to say I swore at him then. "Not that one," I told him. "It's old." I was vain in those days. "Come on, pull me up." Taking my hands in his, he helped me to my feet. "Turn your back," I ordered, although there was nothing to see. I was skin and bone. I found my shoes and padded them with cotton wool against the frost outside. Just as we were about to leave I stopped. "Wait," I said. "I've forgotten something." I found a stub of lipstick in a drawer, discarded since the siege began.'

25

Piskarevskoye lives within me.
Here half the city lie
And they don't know
That rain is falling...
from *Autumn in Piskarevskoye*
Cemetery Sergei Davidov, 1965

A stern grey wall runs along the Avenue of the Unconquered, broken by a wide flight of steps. The trolley-bus deposits us at their foot. We climb the steps to a terrace laid around the tomb of the unknown soldier. The notes of Tchaikovsky's *Pathétique* swirl over the eternal flame, relayed by loudspeakers hung from trees. The terrace is deserted. Aunt Nadya and I stand staring into the flame, a transparent flicker in the sunlight. My eyes sting.

Lena sits behind us on a stone bench. She has remained mute all morning.

Beyond the terrace is a cemetery. On either side of a poplar-lined avenue are rows of grass-covered tumuli – mass graves marked with simple stone plaques: *1942,*

1943… There are many for each year. Above the dates stars are carved for soldiers and oak leaves for civilians.

'600,000 siege dead lie here,' says Aunt Nadya.

We follow the avenue to the foot of a giant wreath-bedecked statue of Mother Russia. The words of the poet Olga Bergholtz are engraved on its base:

Here lie citizens of Leningrad –
Men, women and children
Beside them soldiers of the Red Army
They gave their lives defending you, Leningrad
Cradle of the revolution
Let no one forget, let nothing be forgotten

A wedding party appears on the terrace behind us, posing for photographs. They descend the steps and make their way along the avenue towards Mother Russia. The bride's dress is looped into a crinoline; her starched veil spreads out behind her. In her wake a mini-skirted bridesmaid wobbles bravely on white stilettos. The groom and best man have the cropped hair and wide-shouldered suits of racketeers. It is at least a quarter of a mile from the terrace to the memorial. The party mounts the plinth to lay the bridal bouquet.

I brush a tear from my eye.

'Communist propaganda,' snorts Aunt Nadya as we walk away. 'All this cradle of the revolution crap.'

'I am touched to see the young honour the war dead.'

'The Communists appropriated our siege experience and rewrote it.'

'A lot of people need to believe the myth.' Lena speaks for the first time.

'Because they cannot face themselves,' says Aunt Nadya.

Lena turns to me. 'You see, it's all we ever heard about the siege while I was growing up – in books, films, speeches, at school…'

'Whereas the truth is we all did things that made

us ashamed,' her aunt interrupts. 'We had to in order to survive. We want to be saints but we are not.' Her voice is gruff. 'There was one incident – I don't often talk about it – when I was walking home at dusk, exhausted.' She lights a cigarette. 'It was a time when people were afraid to be out on the streets alone. I came to a crossroads. Two girls were in front of me. One of them had collapsed in the snow and the other was trying to lift her up. "Help me, help me lift my sister," she pleaded as I approached. But I feared that if I bent down I would fall too and no one would come by who would help us up again. "I have a sister too," I whispered. "We are alone." I walked on.'

A stream of smoke curls from her nostrils. 'That was what the siege meant – making choices like that. You had to live with those choices for the rest of your life.'

Lena picks up her bag. 'I've had enough of this place. I'll wait for you in the café across the road, opposite the entrance.'

She strides off.

'Leave her,' says Aunt Nadya. 'She finds it difficult to be here, that's all.'

We sit down on a bench under the trees. A little way off a man paints at an easel; an old lady knits on the next bench while her companion dozes over a newspaper. A blackbird sings from a branch above our heads. I close my eyes and inhale the sweet scent of peonies.

It would be hard to come here in autumn.

'Don't forget the myth was not just harmless propaganda. After the war they started to persecute those who helped keep the city alive,' says Aunt Nadya.

'Like banning Arkadii Kotlyarsky's saxophone, for example?'

'And worse.'

A column of ants swarms between the legs of the bench and disappears into the tumulus behind us.

'People debate whether Stalin was responsible for more atrocities than Hitler,' I say, 'whether Communism was worse than fascism.'

'A particularly facile comparison,' Aunt Nadya retorts. 'And completely beside the point. As I told you at the Smolensk cemetery, our war was not for an ideology but for survival. Our city, its culture, our way of life, everything we stood for, was under attack. The *blokadniki* – most of us at least and even if only subconsciously – were fighting for more than ourselves as individuals, and that is what kept us alive. Despair is infectious, but so is hope.'

She sighs. 'But this city is not what it was. After the war more and more country people came to live here. The best of these had died during collectivisation – although you still find truly wise people in remote villages. We saw the rise of a new class – the technical intelligentsia. The New Russians of their day.'

Her tone is dismissive. 'The name speaks for itself. They were usually Party members or they had Party connections. They were qualified, they had skills, but they were quite a different breed.

'The fact is, Stalin tried to destroy us. He feared this city as a crucible of dissent. He feared the intelligentsia. That's why he was prepared to sacrifice us.'

She grinds her cigarette stub under the toe of her boot. 'Those intelligentsia that he had not managed to kill off in the purges were the first to be sent to the front. They used to joke that people who wore glasses should be careful. Then he began to worry – he realised that they could be useful for propaganda purposes. Shostakovich started off on fire watch duty, then he was evacuated to Kuibyshev. Akhmatova was flown to Tashkent.

'But Stalin didn't destroy all of us. Nor did Hitler. Let's see what democracy will achieve.'

We walk off between the mounds towards the farthest reaches of the cemetery. A wagtail skips ahead over the tumuli, white tail streaks flashing.

'Nadezhda Ivanovna,' I say. 'I wanted to ask you something.'

She inclines her head.

'What if you had not gone to the Musical Comedy with your friend?'

'I might have lasted a couple more weeks.'

We have reached the edge of the cemetery. The mass graves give way to individual plots marked with Orthodox crosses.

'A few years ago,' I say, 'I knew a woman whose parents were killed by a bomb during the siege. She was rescued and evacuated to a children's home in Samara. When she grew up she joined the circus as a trapeze artist. After she had a child she retired from the circus, but in her mind she never left it.'

For thirty years Larisa extended her hands through holes in a protective screen to reach the missile assembly line. Ivan told me that explosions were frequent. Many workers were injured. Larisa had a habit of wiggling her fingers in front of her face as she talked, as though delighted to still have them all.

'The circus, the theatre, the orchestra – we needed them,' Aunt Nadya murmurs.

'Yet when the curtain fell you had to go out onto the street again.'

'Yes, but we had been reminded of the possible.'

Her face brightens. 'Olga Bergholtz expressed it well – you know that her husband died of starvation? Yet she wrote that grief and happiness were like two trees growing together, their roots and crowns intermingled. She said that there were times during the siege when she knew such happiness that her grandchildren would envy her.'

A woman stands with her forehead pressed against a silver birch tree. In this pagan grove tree trunks are decorated with photos – some in oval frames, others exposed to the elements, corners curling. The Seriozhas and Kolyas who never came home gaze out from faded pictures hanging high up the trunks. Rainwashed messages are pinned to the base of the trees, tied together with bouquets of dead flowers.

26

I was no hero
I did not thirst for glory, or for medals.
I breathed one breath with all the Leningraders
I did not play the hero – I simply lived.
Olga Bergholtz

He sits with his back to me, facing out towards the Gulf, sticks propped against the arm of his bench. The wind catches a lock of white hair, making it spiral like a wisp of smoke above his head.

I walk around the bench to greet him.

A pink glow suffuses Dmitriev's face. 'I sensed it was you. Sit down.' He pats the bench beside him.

Crows peck at crumbs scattered around his feet.

'I came to say goodbye.'

He claps his hands. 'That's all. Shoo. Fly away. I'll bring you more tomorrow.'

The air fills with wings.

'So you are leaving?'

'Yes.'

'But you will come back.'

'I hope so.'

'Leningrad has changed,' he sighs.

'So they tell me.'

'Before the war it was different. These days Nevsky looks like Broadway. But still, this city is unique. There is nowhere else like it.'

We sit in silence, watching the hydrofoil curve out from the Tyutchev bridge towards Kronstadt.

'When war broke out I was over there.' He tilts his head towards the western horizon. 'On the Hanko peninsula.'

A pigeon lands on the arm of the bench. One of its legs is injured, the claw bent backwards. Dmitriev places a crumb on his palm. 'That's my beauty.' The pigeon lurches onto his hand. 'It knows me. I come here every day.

'We were finally evacuated from Hanko by convoy. Along the way our ships were blown up by mines, bombed by German planes... thousands of sailors drowned.'

I wonder if it is they who draw him to the Gulf each day.

'I reached the city happy to be alive. We had had no news while on Hanko. We did not know that Leningrad was starving.'

'The first people we saw were a crowd of women who had come down to the pier to meet us. How they heard of our arrival I don't know. I was shocked at the sight of them. One approached me. Her eyes were hollow; she clutched at the wall as she moved. "Dear sailor," she said, "Give me a crust of bread, just a crust..."'

A seagull perches on the arm of our bench, eyeing us inquisitively. 'Nothing today,' says Dmitriev. It opens its beak and screeches.

'I had brought cans of meat with me, sugar, vodka

and bread. I undid my rucksack and gave the woman a whole loaf. She turned away quickly, without a word, clasping it to her breast. Perhaps she feared I might want something in return.

'I saw people collapsing, dropping in the streets. I thought this must be the end.'

'But you survived.'

'We survived.'

He turns to me, his eyes a reflection of the sea. 'And you found answers to your questions?'

'More than that, I learned not to fear asking them.'

'Good.' He is silent for a few moments. 'That is good. You know, we have very similar professions. I can't speak about writing but after sixty-eight years I love acting more than ever. When you appear before the public you experience an overwhelming compulsion to surprise, challenge, evoke emotion...'

'... and tell a story.' I finish for him.

He laughs. 'It is the most intense happiness.'

The sun beats down on our heads. Grey concrete blocks stretch along the waterfront and into the distance. The streets are almost deserted.

'On days of performances,' he continues, 'I could scarcely eat. From morning onwards I accumulated my part, drop by drop.'

Canute-like, he stretches an arm towards the waves. 'This arm belongs to me.' He rotates his wrist. 'I am well-acquainted with it. But on stage I have to play so that I don't recognise my own limbs. And that has nothing to do with costume and make-up.

'As for emotions, well, you have to experience them, to know grief for example, to recognise its forms.'

'They must have been intense during the war.'

'Oh, the war came later. During my childhood I saw people dying of starvation.'

'Here?'

'By the Volga. I grew up in a small town.' A pause. 'And later they took my father away.' His voice is flat.

'To a camp?'

'Ten years without right of correspondence.'

Which means he was shot.

'People kept their distance. I was the son of an Enemy of the People. I learned to take care of myself, to milk a cow, ride a horse... As I said, you accumulate emotion during the course of your life. You accumulate and transform it.' Dmitriev's eyes gleam. 'And then the war... You know, it was incredibly useful to me as an actor. It was such a rich source of material. I watched people change around me. They were living according to different laws. Probably the most important thing is the eyes, you remember how they change in fear, in greed...

'Let me give you an instance.' His deep voice carries along the back of the wooden bench and reverberates within my chest. 'It is night on the Finnish front. Clouds obscure the moon. A young lieutenant, Seriozha Gusin, is my guide. He is a jolly, fair-haired lad from Leningrad. He leads me down a narrow pathway, leaping from boulder to boulder. "Come on, quickly," he urges. "There are snipers all around."

'Crack! An explosion bursts nearby. Seriozha falls to the ground. I run up to him. His brain oozes from a hole in his head. His lips twitch. There is nothing I can do. I bend over and watch as his life ebbs away. Some part of me stands outside myself, like a camera, recording every detail.'

Dmitriev's eyes are distant. 'As I talk to you now I can see that poor lieutenant's eyes, his smile... At the end Seriozha looked like a small boy.'

The Gulf is choppy today, white horses crest its waves. A little cutter sails close to where we sit, a rainbow held in its spray.

'One of our writers,' I say, 'Graham Greene was his name, spoke of the sliver of ice in the heart.'

'The detachment of the observer?'

'Yes,' I reply, 'but it's not really ice, is it?'

Dmitriev shakes his head. 'The observer merely records, I wanted to transform.'

He sighs. 'Later I went to the lieutenant's address in Leningrad. An old woman opened the door. "Is this the home of Lieutenant Gusin?" I asked and saw her eyes widen in fear. "I am his mother," she replied. I saw then that she was only about forty years old. "He's alive and well and sends his love," I said, and left before she could offer me anything to eat or drink.'

Dmitriev picks up his sticks. 'Since that time, over the years, Gusin has returned. There are so many characters in here.' He taps his chest. 'An enormous cast. They all come back.'

⚶

Lena tells me that Volodya was sent to a psychiatric unit on Vasilievsky Island. 'He was taking morphine. He told Osman that some medical technicians stole it from a clinic and supplied him. He decided to stop. Osman used his connections to get him into the hospital and now he is responding well to treatment. Osman and I are going to take him out to spend the weekend with Naima in her dacha. Would you like to come?'

Naima has not the slightest interest in poetry. I am certain she will do Volodya good. 'Yes, I'd love to.'

The red brick hospital building bears a close resemblance to the Kresty prison; the security guard breathes vodka fumes as he admits us. Lena and I wait downstairs while Osman ascends to Volodya's ward. I look up through layers of wire mesh safety netting that stretch across each level of the stairwell. A patient in pyjama bottoms shuffles past, clutching a jam jar of water. Urine trickles from under a toilet door. Someone has placed a jar of daisies on the windowsill of the waiting-room.

There are purple rings around Volodya's eyes but he manages a wan smile when he sees us. Outside the hospital Osman flags down a Lada. He haggles with the driver and we squash in. We drive out past dusty factories and housing estates built on churned-up wasteland. Turning off the main highway, the car bounces down a dirt track past wooden cottages set in vegetable plots.

Naima's dacha stands out amongst its ramshackle neighbours. Its façade gleams with strips of pink plastic cladding. Inside, a red tartan three-piece suite is still covered in protective polythene. Above the sofa hangs a gilt-framed landscape in crude oils. Tiny chips of amber are scattered over it in representation of autumn leaves.

'She is a collector,' says Osman. 'Let's sit in the garden.'

We perch on a log beneath an apple tree, listening to the hum of bees and the distant chatter of neighbours. Volodya does not speak but I sense his tension ebb. Mine too.

Bicycle brakes squeak and the gate swings open. Naima appears in an orange tracksuit and flowered headscarf, wheeling an ancient bike. She smells overpoweringly of fish.

'Did you have a successful day?' asks Osman

'Sold them all. Fifteen roubles a kilo.' She beams and embraces each of us in turn. 'My neighbour is a keen fisherman,' she explains to me. 'I help him out. How are you Volodya, my darling?'

'Better. Better. But I was thinking…'

'Then stop it. Thinking is bad for the complexion –

gives you wrinkles.' She strokes his cheek. 'Come on, I want you to see my flowers.' She leads us around the garden. We admire a profusion of marrows, peas and raspberries. 'Look at these chrysanthemums. I used to grow poppies too. Huge ones. Purple, red and pink. But I had to stop as junkies kept breaking the fence to steal them. Girls, would you like a bath? I've heated the water.'

Without waiting for a reply, she ushers us down the garden path towards a shed that I had assumed was the outdoor toilet. Naima heaves open the door and I inhale the smell of wet birch leaves and wood smoke. 'Excuse me girls, it's like a collective farmer's bath house. I haven't got around to improving it yet.'

For that I am thankful. 'Towels are on the peg, girls. *Slyogkym parom.*'

With that universal Russian bathhouse wish 'may your steam be light,' Naima shuts the door on us.

'She normally makes her *samogon* in here,' says Lena. 'Must have run out of sugar.'

Moonshine. I wonder if there is no end to her enter-prise. She and Ivan would have found a lot in common. Superficially at least. For unlike Ivan, Naima believes in recycling her good fortune.

We strip off and lie on a long wooden bench, taking it in turns to flail each other with bundles of birch leaves. I never understand why non-Russians assume this to be an act of masochism. It is the leaves that make contact with the flesh, not the twigs. They patter against my thighs, releasing a smell of woods after summer rain.

Lena and I sit side by side, flesh gleaming pink through the steam.

'I can't think of anywhere on this earth I would rather be.'

'I'm glad.' Lena pulls up her knees to her chest. 'You know, when the siege began to affect you, I worried.'

'I didn't mean to…'

She cuts me off. 'And then we watched you begin to understand…'

I slosh more water onto the stone floor. Lena's face glows, making her appear ten years younger.

'My research affected you too, didn't it?' I ask her.

She picks up a leaf-bundle and starts to work on the soles of my feet. 'Yes. Well it forced me to poke around my own family's entrails. It was sore at first, but I'm better for it.'

Leaves patter against my calves until I can almost see the blood surging through my veins.

'I was surprised how open people are with you,' she says after a while, 'and touched. The *blokadniki* are not always so willing to talk. I've interpreted for western journalists and they usually only get the official line.'

'I can understand them being wary.'

Lena flails harder. 'In the west I noticed how people are fascinated by tragedy. Your press revolves around it. Your relish for it shocked me – perhaps it reinforces your frantic pursuit of pleasure.'

'But I do not feel like a voyeur here,' I say. 'It feels more like looking into a mirror. All the while I keep asking myself how might I have behaved in those circumstances.'

'Well?'

'Impossible to say.'

Lena throws a bucket of cold water over me, and then douses herself. We dress and go outside to dry off in the sun.

Naima beams at me, pinches my arm and tells me I'm pretty. 'If you're not careful you'll catch a husband.'

Volodya smiles. I tell him he looks much better.

'I made my choice in the end.'

Naima squeezes his hand. 'We are proud of you, sweetheart.'

'I used to blame circumstance,' he explains. 'I felt it was the fault of the world if my poems were not published. In reality I was a very great victim. My parents, by the way, were *blokadniki*.

'That evening at your flat, Lena, was the last straw. The people who gave away their bread in camps were not victims; the *blokadniki* were not victims, so why should I be?

'The difference between then and now,' he continues, 'was that in the siege everything was clear, you had an external enemy to fight. But a little Hitlerite had crept inside me. He would whisper lies until I believed him, until I confused his voice with my own.'

Volodya seizes a cane from the tomato bed beside him and traces a circle in the dust.

'I laid siege to myself.'

'You don't need to stick needles into your arm to do that,' says Osman.

'Of course not,' agrees Volodya. 'Despair took hold long ago, before I picked up a needle; morphine seemed like a rational way of treating it.'

Lena sighs. 'To some degree we all lay siege to ourselves.'

I think of the winter when she worked in the street market until her aunt rescued her.

Naima emerges from her dacha carrying a dish of raspberries and a jug of sour cream. 'Children!' she calls. I look around and then realise she means us.

'Perhaps not all of us,' I say, nodding in Naima's direction.

We laugh.

'What's so funny?' asks Naima, handing us each a spoon. 'How pleasant it is to hear your laughter. Does my plants good.'

Later, as dusk falls, Osman, Lena and I take our

leave. Naima stands at the gate of her palace, waving us down the lane. Small dogs slip beneath gates to bark at our heels. Giant sunflowers bow their heads over picket fences, as though in farewell.

27

1942.
Spring brings with it –
not swallows, but trams.
Nikolai Tikhonov

This tram is old, a wartime relic. The doors at either end are open, allowing a breeze to play through the vehicle. It is Sunday and the streets are deserted of all but the very poor and the very drunk. Everyone who can has gone to their dachas in the countryside. A slatted bench runs the length of the car. I have it to myself, with Boldyrev's ghost beside me. On his way to work, he is absorbed in reading the high society antics of *Lady Rose's Daughter* by Mrs Humphrey Ward. He finds this type of literature particularly effective in shutting out the horrors of his daily existence.

The tram halts at a crossing. A headscarved woman sweeps the cobbles in front of a French fashion house, just as her great-grandmother might have done a hundred years ago, on the far side of revolution, terror and war. At some level, society has scarcely changed.

The conductor plumps down beside me and smiles. My heart sinks. Usually men in Petersburg leave me alone, unless they are drunk.

'Another hot day,' he remarks, taking out a handkerchief and mopping his brow. At least he doesn't smell of vodka.

'Yes.'

'You are not from here?'

'No, England.'

'Are you married? Children?'

'No.'

I brace myself.

The conductor slaps his leg. 'How marvellous to be so independent. You come all this way. I would like to travel too, to see the world. Still, this is a good job. You meet all sorts of people.'

'It must be.'

'Did you know that Petersburg has more trams than any other city in the world?'

'No I didn't.'

'More than Melbourne, Vienna or Philadelphia. We bring these old ones out from the museum for a run. For an airing, like retired workhorses. Only on summer Sundays, so they don't get overloaded.'

'I was wondering, do you think this tram ran through the siege?'

'So you are interested in that…' His smile fades. 'Well, probably. Although they stopped running during that first winter. They stood abandoned in the streets. But later in spring we got them going again. Passersby wept when they saw the first trams. People loved to hear their bells clang – it cheered them, helped them believe in victory.'

Gostinny Dvor. 'Bloody Corner. There was a terrible strike here.' He shakes his head. 'A direct hit on a tram queue. Dozens killed. They had to move the stops to protect them from shelling. The Germans knew their positions. We lost 150 vehicles. Hundreds of drivers and conductors died or were killed at the front.'

We halt again. A crowd surges towards the doors. 'How much?' a man shouts.

'Two roubles.'

'Two roubles! And they expect us to ride on that clapped-out thing!' As one, the group ebbs to the kerb to wait for a modern made-in-Czechoslovakia vehicle.

The tram deposits me on Turgenev Square. The conductor waves as it rattles off.

I wave back. The bell clangs and I turn down a side street towards Valentina Pavlovna's flat.

❧

A man gazes down from her walls: dark brows, generous, curving lips – I wonder how I missed him before. 'My husband, Boris Nikolaevich.' Valentina Pavlovna picks up an intricately carved wooden box from a shelf. 'He made this. I used to say he had golden hands.' She lifts the lid of the box to reveal three medals lying inside. 'Those were his.'

Her voice is light, almost girlish. 'Perhaps no other woman has received letters such as those he wrote before we were married. He used to say that in me he saw a soul of great beauty.' She smiles. 'I wanted to show you one of his letters but wasn't able to find it before you arrived. He wrote *I love you with all your wounds…*'

A raw spot within me quivers. My soul, Dmitriev would say.

'Boris Nikolaevich helped me learn to live after

my injury. He was only sixty-three when he died of a heart attack.'

She closes the lid of the box and replaces it on the shelf. 'Then in 1987 I found my doctor again. After forty years. The man who saved my life. We talked and cried together. After that we used to phone each other every day. He died a few years ago.

'These days my son and grandson visit me, although not too often as they live in the North, in Murmansk. But I have my good kind Russian neighbours.'

As she opens the door Valentina says shyly, 'You admired the wool rug on my bed. I was wondering if you would give me your address in England so I could send it to you.'

I descend the dank stairwell for the last time.

'You have to be careful,' explains Lena when I reach home. 'If you admire something people will want you to have it. They believe that without it you will suffer. And they don't want to be responsible for that.'

❧

'I love the city on Sundays,' I say. 'When everyone has gone to their dachas. It is so empty, so peaceful.'

I am out shopping with Aunt Nadya. She likes to wander around the new supermarkets examining imported goods in their shiny packaging. I notice she doesn't buy much.

'It reminds me of Leningrad after that first winter,' she remarks, squinting at a tin of Polish coffee as though it were rat poison. 'By summer 1942 there were only a million of us left; perhaps not even that. So many people had died, and most of the surviving children had been evacuated. The city changed then, we were souls rattling inside an ancient, emaciated body. After that long winter cooped up in dark rooms behind boarded-up windows we weren't used to having so much space around us; it made us dizzy. The topography of the city had changed. When I walked the shattered streets it was as though my feet were tracing the city's skeleton: Nevsky was its spine, with Sadovaya, Liteiny, the Fontanka, Moika and Griboyedov Canal its ribs. The wind whistled through empty buildings – some had no more than their façades left standing. So many buildings had been shelled. When fires started we had no water to put them out. Whole apartment blocks burned for days. They lay in piles of rubble everywhere, like collapsed organs.

'Oh it was a strange time, but very beautiful, in summer the northern lights played over us.' She holds up a plastic bottle of Hungarian mayonnaise. 'Tell me, is this meant to be food or some kind of cleaning fluid?'

'Probably not much difference,' I say. 'But tell me more about the city.'

'Well, of course there were pockets of fat left, congealed and rancid. In Smolny, the Big House – the canteens where police and government officials ate – there was food. Throughout the siege they had food. They tried to keep it quiet, but we all knew. Special consignments were brought in. You could see the officials, with their fat cheeks and dead eyes.'

Vishnevskaya wrote that once, during the siege, her Communist father, who had abandoned her shortly after her birth, invited her to have a meal with his new family. The woman he lived with looked at the emaciated Vishnevskaya and asked, 'But why is she so scrawny?' And this was when the streets were full of corpses. Perhaps some of the well-fed cultivated blindness, for fear that they might not survive if they saw the reality under their noses.

'It must have been hard. Knowing there was food.'

Aunt Nadia shrugs. 'What could we do? We were used to it, don't forget, we had lived through the 1930s as well. Those in power were no longer were able to surprise us.'

My second visit to Leningrad was in late 1990. Economic reform had created 'supply problems' resulting in long queues for food and near-empty shops. Once again people had been issued with ration cards. And yet still there were pockets of fat. Black marketeers were enriching themselves just as they had done during the siege. As a foreigner I was permitted to use the so-called dollar shops. These only accepted foreign currency, which was illegal for ordinary Soviet citizens to hold. I took orders from friends, had my passport checked inside the shop, and with an excruciating sense of injustice bought a selection of foodstuffs that were unobtainable for ninety-nine per cent of the citizens of the country in which I was a guest.

'And how did those government officials feel, feeding themselves while their fellow citizens starved?'

'Scared out of their wits. Scared of losing their meal tickets. Scared of facing the firing squad.'

She thrusts a Snickers bar back into a box of western confectionery. 'Many of them were executed after the war – but not for that. They were accused of being British agents and so on. Another Kremlin power struggle. Come on. Let's go to the market and buy some real food.'

❦

Raindrops tap against the window. The weather is turning. 'Cranes will soon be flying,' says Lena. 'The first sign of autumn, the sight of them always makes me cry.'

Before my return to England I am taking a trip with her and Aunt Nadya across Lake Ladoga. Lena kneels on the floor packing clothes into a holdall. She suddenly springs to her feet and crosses to the airing cupboard. 'Take it.' She thrusts a *Minzdrav* sheet into my hand. 'A souvenir.'

'Oh but…' I protest.

Lena raises a hand. 'Plenty more where they came from. My aunt works at the hospital, remember?'

I catch my breath. 'You mean Aunt Nadya…?' *Biznes* is one thing, pilfering another. Somehow I can't imagine her stuffing her briefcase with sheets from the hospital stores.

Lena smiles. 'No one wants these any more.'

I phone the *blokadniki* to say goodbye.

Arkadii Kotlyarsky: 'Come back to see us. You will always be welcome.'

Ksenia Matus: 'May you find a husband and be happy.'

Ivan Dmitriev: 'I still have a picture of you in my mind. You are a very light and original person.'

I have bought myself a striped sailor's *tel'nyashka* in his honour. My Ivan would have been horrified.

In the evening, after we finish packing our bags, Lena and I sit out on the balcony watching dusk fall. Swallows congregate on telephone wires above our heads. Random oblongs of light appear in the block opposite, shadows flickering within them. A violin is tuned, plates clatter, the air is rich with the scent of grilling meat. Voices drift up from below, urgent whisperings, a scuffle: 'Masha, don't go, wait…' Beyond these, from out of the dark, the faint sound of an accordion.

28

Fiery and triumphant city
Built on corpses; built on bones
Maximilian Voloshin

Rain has left a damp autumnal smell in the air. Chestnut leaves are already crinkling with rust. We take a bus to the Neva river station. It is Sunday and few people are about. At the back of the bus sits a young man with clumsily tattooed hands. My skin pricks as the *zek* twitches and swears beneath his breath.

The tram shudders to a halt. Its doors slam open. A walnut hand grips the rail. A scarved head appears and falls away again. The *zek* is on his feet and holding out his arms to the *babushka*. He hauls her into the bus and guides her to a seat across the aisle, then collapses back into his own, spitting curses at an unseen foe.

At the river station we join the inevitable queue to collect our tickets. It is almost departure time. We hurry across the road and along the quay towards our ship. 'Run, girls!' a group of idling sailors shouts. Aunt Nadya laughs while Lena slows to a dignified pace, the chiffon of her sundress clinging to her body as she walks. The officer who hands us onto the gangplank stares at her with open admiration. She doesn't notice; I suspect she never does.

❧

Middle-aged ladies with imposing hairstyles are already parading on the deck of the *Kronstadt,* arm in arm with their stout partners, former Party officials, at a guess. A Georgian family bedecked in gold jewellery photograph each other, their children's faces as calm and dark as icons. A flash, a shriek of laughter and they scatter, black locks splayed in the wind. A young couple in shiny clothes approach us. 'Please ladies, take our picture together,' the boy asks in a country accent. They pose, his arm stiff across his beloved's shoulders, taking care not to crumple the frill of her collar.

'I'm going down to my cabin, girls. I have reading to catch up on.' Aunt Nadya disappears, leaving Lena and me on deck. We lean on the ship's rail, watching the crowd bustle along the quayside. Brakes screech below us. A tiny battered Zaporozhets has pulled up. The passenger door opens and Naima Suleimanovna squeezes out, clutching a bouquet of purple dahlias.

'They've come to see us off.' Lena waves.

Naima catches sight of us and waves the bouquet in response. She staggers along the gangplank in her high heels, holding up her skirt, the solemn Osman in her wake. She plants multiple kisses on our cheeks and thrusts the flowers into my arms.

'Goodbye girls.'

'We're only going for three days,' I whisper in English to Lena.

'It's the drama,' Lena whispers back. 'And she needs to express her love.'

Osman has been standing to one side, regarding Lena intently. Now he takes my hand and kisses it.

'Bon voyage.'

A blast of the ship's whistle and an announcer instructs all non-passengers to disembark. There is a rush for the gang-plank. Naima ensures that she bumps into the most handsome of the sailors. He bows to her in mock-apology.

Once ashore she stops and waves back to us. We watch as a small crowd gathers around her. 'She's found her audience,' says Lena. 'She's telling them about you.'

A loudspeaker crackles into life above our heads. A woman's voice, redolent with optimism, relays facts and figures. 'Ladoga is the largest lake in Europe...' It is a voice from the Soviet past.

'Together we stride forward into a radiant future,' Lena and I chant in unison. 'Tomorrow will be better than today.'

The voice is cut off in mid-sentence by the ship's hooter. The *Kronstadt* swings out from the river station and into the Neva. We sail away from the city, from the burning forest, past fields and wooden dachas. Groups of picnickers raise their bottles in greeting. A bonfire glimmers through the violet dusk. Shadowy figures stand around it as though at a witches' sabbat. Ahead of us, on a rocky island in the middle of the water lies a squat stone fortress, ghostly in the white midnight.

'Oreshek – our eternal jail,' says Lena. 'Tsar Peter imprisoned his wife Yevdotiya here, the Decembrists were held here, Lenin's brother was hanged here. It held out against the Germans for 500 days.'

Some time during the night I awaken, cold for the first time in weeks. I shiver. We must be crossing the ice road, our hull drifting over sunken lorries and the scattered bones of those who never made it to the far shore.

I glance across at Lena. She lies as still as a stone saint on a tomb, her ribs outlined beneath the sheet, her nose a gaunt ridge between pockets of shadow.

White glimmers beneath her lids.

'You need more rest,' I say.

'Don't worry about me.'

'But I do.'

'I'm strong. You see, most of us Russians are accustomed to material hardship. Perhaps we are too ready to accept it; perhaps we should strive harder to improve our situation.'

'Many do – these days.'

She snorts. 'Let's leave the New Russians out of it. In the end it is not the material that enriches life. Joy lies in the irrational, the spontaneous.'

I groan. 'Don't talk to me about the irrational. Your daily life drives me nuts. The queues, the public rudeness, everything breaking down…'

'That's not what I meant.' Her voice is weary. 'You need to venture beyond your Aristotelian logic.'

'Meaning?'

'Meaning that faith grows in direct proportion to life's challenges.' She sits upright now, fully awake. 'You see, if you lie back in comfort faith will never be more than a lovely, distant mirage, a beguiling consolation. When you go through hellfire and high water, brass trumpets and devil's teeth, as we say here, it becomes a daily working reality.' She reaches over to the table between our berths and pours some *Borzhomi* water into our glasses.

'I am still not sure what you are getting at.'

'I'll give you an illustration: I went to a conference in Finland last year. I made a good friend there. She cried as she saw me onto the plane, partly because she was sad that I was leaving but also because I was returning to poor deprived Russia, as she saw it. I could not explain to her that I was glad. It was beyond her comprehension.

'You see, in many ways life is hard for you in the materialist West. You have so many distractions.'

'They didn't have many in the siege,' I say.

'No, life was reduced to its bare bones: were you going to eat that day or not?'

'That was a very material question.'

'Material yes, but the answer lay with the spirit. Unless you had faith you died. Of course for most people it was not a religious faith, but faith was vital all the same. It was about having the strength to act on that faith – your Professor Tikhvinskii is a splendid example.'

She sighs. 'But for us who come after it is not so straightforward. It is what Volodya was talking about. During the siege you had an external enemy; during the Soviet period too, we had something to fight against. Now many of us feel lost, directionless.

'Sometimes this world feels unreal.' She gestures towards the cabin window. 'As insubstantial as the mist out there. Looking at it reminds me how as I child I felt the dividing line between our world and the next was imperceptibly thin. As though I could just step from one to the other.'

'Like Alice through the Looking Glass?'

'Like Alice.' She slides down into her berth. 'Now let's get some sleep. We arrive early in the morning.'

The ship sails on, northwards.

✣

I awaken to a grey smear on the horizon.

'That's Valaam, the main island,' says Aunt Nadya as we stand on deck after breakfast. You can see the monastery domes on that headland. Invalids were sent here after the war, men who had lost their limbs. It became a convalescent hospital.'

I have a sudden image of Kolya, the Ukrainian soldier befriended by Galina. Perhaps he ended his days in this tranquil place.

Ashore, the Party officials, the Georgians and the country couple assemble beside a gift shop, ready for their guided tour.

'Follow me, girls!' Aunt Nadya plunges into the undergrowth behind the shop. I catch the startled expression of the guide before Lena grabs my hand and pulls me with her. We follow a track through a sunlit wood, past a little wooden chapel, and emerge onto a rocky shore. Seating ourselves on a low cliff, we gaze out over the lake. Below us a pair of monks fish from a rowing boat. Across the channel is an islet covered in pines.

'A hermit lives over there,' says Lena. 'After the collapse of the Soviet Union they let the monks return.'

Beyond the islet the lake spreads out to meet the sky. Lena points to a flat mother-of-pearl streak on the rippled water. 'A god just passed by. That's what the Finns believed. This lake was once a part of Finland. It came back to us after the war.'

She sits in contemplation, chin cupped in her hands, eyes half closed. Out of respect for the holy place we are in she has covered her hair with a scarf. A few strands escape and blow across her face in the warm breeze.

It is as though I am seeing her for the first time.

'This is where you should live,' I say. 'You belong here. As much as the lichen on these rocks.'

She looks up, her face grave. 'I once spent a whole summer at a monastery near Novgorod. We had to work hard digging potatoes but it was the best summer of my life.'

We remain still for a long time, listening to birdsong and the gentle suck of water on rock.

'Do they let you dig potatoes here?' I ask.

'I believe so.'

'Let's stay then. In our free time you can go to church and I'll write. We'll grow old here. We'll forget about the mainland.'

She smiles and replies in English, 'And if one day we remember it, we can communicate by dove.'

We return to the *Kronstadt*, tourists again, photographing each other beneath its white bows.

Once on board Lena wanders off to play a piano she has discovered in the ship's lounge while Aunt Nadya and I go up on deck. We find a couple of chairs and lie back in companionable silence, my precious exercise book on my lap, its pages almost full. The ship heads out into the lake. We watch Valaam disappear over the horizon. Behind us, strains of a Chopin *Nocturne* drift through an open window.

A tern hovers above the deck rail, then shears off and plummets into the water. My mind peels back from the serenity of the evening to the lines of trucks battling through blizzards under strafing and aerial bombardment.

Ladoga is the fourteenth largest lake in the world, an inland sea, its shores invisible to us from this point. The Road of Life cut across the narrowest point at the southern end of the lake, running for twenty miles from

Osinovets on the Leningrad side to landing points on the unoccupied 'mainland', beyond the German lines.

'Nadezhda Ivanovna,' I begin, 'I am grateful to you, all of you…'

She cuts me off. 'People wanted to talk to you. They warmed to you. I sensed they would. They want to talk before it is too late and we are all gone. They want the world to know what human beings are capable of – the best and the worst.'

'They certainly showed me that.'

I remember something else. 'No one showed resentment towards the Germans. No one mentioned that.'

She sits bolt upright in her chair. 'Haven't you understood anything?'

'Sorry?'

'What would be the point of fanning the flames of war for sixty years?

'No, I see. Of course,' I say lamely.

'If you hold onto hatred you are lost, defeated. Hitler fed on fear and hatred; we found another way.'

'I wanted to ask you one more thing,' I say. 'Back in the Smolensk cemetery you spoke about your joy.'

Pulling off her dark glasses, she squints into the sun. 'It's true. Our existence was stripped to its most basic elements. A small pleasure that would go unnoticed in peacetime became enormous. The sight of a blade of grass pushing up through the ground after that first terrible winter was so precious it made me almost drunk with happiness.

'I was young in those days so of course I loved Dostoevsky – I don't read him any more – haven't got the spiritual strength. Ivan Karamazov loved his "sticky little leaves of spring", and the blue sky and life. He loved them "with his inside, with his belly". And so did I. My God, so did I…

'We lived in a state of altered consciousness. You have heard how despair turned people savage, but it worked the other way too. Oh, we saw life with such clarity – all of human life.'

'Once,' I say, 'I received a letter informing me that a friend had fallen to his death. I went into a sort of trance. I stood in the street, a normal London street that I walked every day and probably no longer saw. At that moment I was overcome by its aliveness, its beauty. I heard the birdsong and smelled the spring air as though for the first time. Forgetting myself, I smiled into the faces of passersby. When someone propositioned me I pulled myself together. I went home with an odd feeling of guilt. It was the shock I suppose.'

'It propelled you beyond your self-imposed limits,' says Aunt Nadya. 'Happened to us all the time.'

She sighs. 'These days people have grown lazy. Many live in a state of boredom and discontent – misery you might say. They have become bitter and envious – more conscious of what they lack than what they have. It makes them ill – in my profession I see it all the time. And they think this is the natural state of affairs. They feed off each other. You hear them moaning at the tram stops, in canteens... always blaming someone else. It used to be the Communists...'

She pulls out a compact from her bag and refreshes her lipstick, a luscious cerise that tones with her purple cardigan.

'... And now it's the democrats.' I finish for her. 'It's the same at home too. Insane, when you think of it, in peacetime, among healthy people in a wealthy country...'

She grabs my arm. 'You must not listen to any of it. I am serious. It may not kill you, but it will diminish your life. Lidiya Ginzberg said that one should steer clear of people "who are unhappy on principle". She said it meant more to her to talk with a happy person than with someone of high intelligence... She learned that in the siege and she is right. I am shocked that people find it so easy to make themselves unhappy. It's sheer laziness. Life is a gift.' She smiles at me. 'Don't waste it.'

At seven we head below decks to the dining-room. I am hungry after a day in the fresh air. The restaurant manager, a stout woman with hennaed hair, stops us at the doorway. 'Cabin numbers?' she barks. She goes to her desk, puts on her spectacles and consults a printed list. 'Seats sixty-eight, sixty-nine and seventy.'

'Can't we sit by a window?' I whisper to Lena. The dining-room is half empty.

'No. If we change seats they won't be able to cope.'

'They'll probably throw us out,' says Aunt Nadya with a grin.

A waitress sets plates of meat and potatoes in front of us.

'I asked for fish,' I say.

The girl stares at me as though I were mentally ill. 'These are cutlets.'

'Yes. But I asked for fish. I ordered it last night. The manager told me that if I wanted fish I would have to order it in advance.'

'You are sitting in place sixty-eight,' the waitress replies and struts off down the aisle.

I get up and seek out the manager. She is still poring over her list, ignoring the queue of passengers outside the door.

'Excuse me,' I butt in. 'Last night you told me that if I wanted fish I would have to order it in advance. I did, but the waitress won't serve me.'

The sulky waitress comes over. 'Fish goes to number seventeen. She is in sixty-eight.'

I look around. 'There is no one in seventeen. If I sit there will you bring the fish?'

She avoids my eyes. 'You are in place sixty-eight.'

Desperate now, I employ the only form of *blat* at my disposal – being a foreigner. 'Perhaps I have misunderstood. You see, my language is not so good, and where I come from...'

The manager stares at me as though I were playing a trick on her. She suddenly beams. 'Why didn't you say so? Wait a minute.' She pats my arm. Disappearing into the kitchen, she emerges with a plate of fried fish on a wilted lettuce leaf. She waves me down the aisle ahead of her. Once I am seated she places the food in front of me. 'Bon appetit.'

Lena and her aunt choke into their napkins.

'I don't see what's so funny.' I plunge my knife into the cold fish and then burst out laughing too.

'Last night,' I extract a fishbone from my gum, 'Lena and I were talking about the irrational.'

'There is an internal logic to their system,' says Aunt Nadya. 'It is the way they have always worked.'

'Pushkin said they do it on purpose,' says Lena, 'to relieve the boredom.'

'I didn't mean the dining-room staff,' I say. 'I was thinking about that choir, the one which sang *Ode to Joy*.'

'Preobrazhenskaya. 1941.'

'That concert was bloody irrational. Imagine being a German soldier freezing in a trench and suddenly hearing "*Freude! Freude!*"'

They smile.

'It was what got you through, wasn't it? The starving people who gave away their rations, the poets who wrote by candlelight in freezing flats...'

'Of course,' Aunt Nadya replies as she pours herself more *Borzhomi*. 'We had to go against our instincts, otherwise we would all have ended up savaging each other, gnawing on the bones of corpses.' She raises a glass smeared with crimson lipstick. 'In the end it wasn't the Germans we defeated, it was ourselves. After that the enemy was nothing, a paper tiger...Our own government too.'

Ivan never questioned his instincts. He never acknowledged the hunger that Aunt Nadya, Dmitriev and the others saw in themselves and overcame. He died a stupid unnecessary death, falling from the balcony one night trying to break into his flat after he had locked himself out.

'Are you enjoying your fish?'The young waitress leans over me.

'It's delicious.'

A mouthful of gold teeth flashes at me.

I received the letter early this spring. It arrived on a bright morning that already held the promise of summer. A Russian stamp and unfamiliar handwriting. Sergei, one of Ivan's business partners, had found my address.

The strange thing was, the news scarcely surprised me.

And what about Larisa? I wondered if she would survive the blow. I folded the letter quickly and went out onto the street.

As we file out of the dining-room a young cook emerges from the galley to stare at the foreigner. The restaurant manager bows as we pass.

'Come back and see us again soon.'

'I will.'

29

After a long oblivion
I awaken – all around is quiet
I try to recall where my family have gone
I remember – there was a war.
Which one? And which year is it now –
'Seventeen or 'forty-five?
Above me a sooty vault
And the air in the room is foul.

I don't want to rise from my bed
I know what lies all about
Loneliness everywhere
It fills my house.
I have to begin everything afresh
Seek out new friends
There is my old dance dress
To patch up and mend.
Anna Alexeeva, 5 April 1945 – *Loneliness*

The *Arrow* express pulls into Moscow. There are a few hours to spare before I catch my train home, enough time to visit the crumbling fourteenth-century Novospasskii monastery on the banks of the Moscow river. Foreign Communists lie buried beside it, shot, along with their ideals, during the purges of the 1930s. After the revolution the monastery served as a prison, then a rehabilitation centre for alcoholics. Now its courtyard is tranquil, a haven from the Moscow heat and traffic. I find a bench and lean back; all around me fat bumble bees busy themselves among tall clover.

This summer I feel as though I have looked into a stereoscope like the one I viewed in Samara. Images of horror, starvation, death and cannibalism have been replaced by others of infinite value, whose significance I am only just beginning to assimilate.

Galina Vishnevskaya's words return to me: how she organised vivid mental images of besieged Leningrad until they took on the idiom of the stage. The greatest roles, she stated, demand that the artist accumulate life experience, inner riches. Tamara Petkevich, Ivan Dmitriev and the others not only became reconciled to their experiences, they transcended them.

As I leave the monastery I read a notice pinned to the entrance: *If you buy goods from the USA, Germany, or the United Kingdom you are helping to finance the war against Yugoslavia.*

From the beginning, from my teenage years of reading *War and Peace,* Russia has opened up other perspectives.

As dusk falls I catch a bus to the Belorusskii terminus. The Moscow-Cologne express waits in the pouring rain, uniformed conductors stand by each carriage checking tickets and collecting passports.

The last time I came to Moscow I flew into Sheremetevo airport. Once it distributed free copies of Lenin's *State and Revolution* in the major languages of the world; now it is a designer shopping mall where you can obtain anything but useful information. Russian staff ignored me when I requested directions to my boarding gate. I was rescued by a group of Japanese businessmen.

But the train evokes anticipation and nostalgia. As a child I would read the destination board for the boat train at Victoria station: *Berlin-Warsaw-Moscow;* in those days we travelled as far as Dieppe, but I knew it would only be a matter of time before I went further.

My compartment is already occupied by a dark man in his thirties and a middle-aged woman who introduces herself as Natasha from Kazan. The man clutches a can of beer. 'I can't sleep on these trains,' he grumbles. 'I was with two women all the way up to Moscow and I didn't give them any rest.' My heart sinks. As I make up my bed he turns to Natasha. 'My name is Imam. I was seven years in Afghanistan. An army translator.'

I lie down on my bunk, the lowest in the tier of three. Natasha sleeps in the middle berth. Imam squats on the floor by my pillow, gnawing a chicken leg from a piece of newspaper. He mutters to himself in between bites.

'Shall we get some sleep?' I suggest.

'Why? Are we going anywhere tomorrow?'

I could ask the conductor to change my berth, but that seems too much effort. I give in.

'Where are you from?'

He flashes a gold-toothed smile. 'Daghestan. I am an Avar. I am travelling to Italy to claim political asylum.'

'What from?'

'The fundamentalists caught me drinking a bottle of beer on a bus. They pulled me off and threatened to beat me up. I poured away the beer and they let me go. I went to complain to the local police. They told me to sort it out with the fundamentalists. It's getting worse down there. Fields are destroyed, factories not working. The fundamentalists give food to the poor and call them to prayer. They are winning support.

'There are thirty-eight nationalities in Daghestan. There's a lot of banditry. Particularly the Chechens. They give guns to the young kids.'

'Why will the Italians give you asylum?'

'Because that's where my forefathers come from. The barbarians captured them and carried them off to the Caspian Sea.'

This must have happened back in the Dark Ages – on these grounds I could claim Norwegian asylum on the grounds of Viking ancestry.

We pull into Minsk. Imam alights to go and bargain on the platform with the female vendors. He returns triumphant. 'Three cans of conserved meat – they can't get those in Belarus, they are all shipped to Moscow – for three bottles of vodka.'

Imam disappears with his bottles into the conductor's compartment. With relief I switch on my reading light and pick up Alexeeva's book again.

Grief howls like a dog all night long
Howls and sings in the chimney
I don't even know where your grave is
My only and dearest friend...

She dragged her husband's corpse to the mortuary. She continued to write. She wrote through the death of her son:

Perhaps after another hundred years
Some other Anna will sit and weep over my poem

Anna Alexeeva's heart finally gave out in July 1945, two months after the war in Europe ended.

I doze through Poland. At Poznan Central I glimpse some ragged men sleeping on benches, beer cans scattered beneath them. Natasha's eyes widen. 'Do you have homeless people in the West too?'

'I am afraid so.'

She shakes her head. 'We never believed that. Anything our Communist government told us had to be a lie.'

That evening, as we reach Frankfurt-am-Oder on the German border Imam reappears, dishevelled and reeking of spirits.

The German border guards take one look at his passport and haul him off the train. I watch him walk down the platform, clutching his bottle, flanked by uniforms. He waves without turning round.

'He's got a weakness for the bottle,' says Natasha, while she gathers up her luggage in order to change trains. 'He's been in Afghanistan…'

The train enters another night. The overhead light dims to a ghostly green flicker. By the glow of this railway aurora borealis I see that I am not alone. *Blokadniki* are crowded into the compartment with me, squatting on the floor and swinging their legs from the upper berths, as though excited to be leaving Russia together.

'Your life won't be the same now.' Olga Firsovna waves a cigarette.

'Are you ready for the struggle ahead?' asks Professor Tikhvinskii, standing sentry by the door.

'Here's a piece of bread to keep beside your pillow.' Arkadii reaches down from the berth above mine.

An unknown woman knocks on the door. Her hair is dishevelled and her eyes red. 'Is my son in here? He is coming home from the front. We are expecting him any day now.'

The train shudders to a halt and my companions vanish. I lift the corner of the blind. *Berlin Ostbahnhof.* Doors slam; announcements reverberate down the platform. *Achtung! Ankunft des Zuges aus Moskau am Bahnsteig Fünf...* I try to recapture sleep in the hope that my companions will show themselves again. But in vain.

The *blokadniki* are gone; they will never leave me.

AFTERWORD

As the years go by news reaches me of the deaths of *blokadniki*: Ksenia Matus, Yevgenii Lind, Ivan Dmitriev... Aunt Nadya died peacefully in 2009. Lena left St Petersburg and found a home working in a children's colony deep in the Russian countryside.

In the blazing summer of 2003 builders began work in the London flat beneath mine. One day, tired of the hammering and drilling, I grabbed my laptop and headed outside to seek a more peaceful place to work. I stopped in my tracks outside the neighbour's door. A Russian song – an old romance – was playing inside. An unusual choice for builders, I thought. On an impulse I knocked. A young man in a tool belt appeared. 'Are you Russian?' I blurted out, looking into pale blue eyes set above wide cheekbones.

The man smiled and held out a huge hand. 'Andrei.'

'Caroline.'

'How come you speak Russian?'

'I lived there for a while. In Samara, Petersburg... Whereabouts are you from?'

'I grew up in Ukraine but my mother is Siberian. My grandmother was born in Leningrad.'

I shivered despite the heat. 'And was she a *blokadnitsa*?'

He nodded. 'She was evacuated across the Road of Life.'

The carpenter and I sat down on the stairs and began to talk.

Andrei and I married in 2004.

CONTEXT

THE SIEGE OF LENINGRAD

On 22 June 1941 Hitler launched operation Barbarossa, the invasion of the Soviet Union. Leningrad was the USSR's second city with a population of three million. All able-bodied persons were immediately enlisted to build anti-tank fortifications, but by the end of July German forces had penetrated the city's outer defences and cut the Leningrad-Moscow railway. By September they had reached the edge of Leningrad. They were held off by further fortifications and 200,000 Red Army troops.

When the initial attack on Leningrad failed, Nazi generals appealed to Hitler for permission to besiege the city in order free up panzer units needed elsewhere on the Eastern Front. They were also afraid of contracting diseases such as typhus if they went into the city. Hitler agreed (see Appendix 1). German forces were joined by Finnish troops advancing from the north down the Karelian isthmus. The Germans were determined to destroy the city rather than accept surrender. Their decision was influenced by heavy losses incurred in the occupation of Kiev after the NKVD mined the city centre with explosives.

Several hundred thousand citizens had been evacuated from Leningrad in the summer; these were replaced by refugees from the surrounding countryside fleeing the German advance. Three quarters of the city's industrial plants were evacuated. The rest were converted to armaments production and continued to function during the siege. They were staffed by women, adolescents and the elderly, often working in freezing conditions under open roofs.

During the first winter of the siege all domestic electricity, heating and water had to be shut down. Public transport stopped running until the end of the siege, apart from some tramlines which resumed operation in the spring of 1942.

Food shortages were exacerbated by the bombing of the Badayev stores on the night of 8 September 1941. By mid-November rations had fallen to 125 grammes of bread a day for non-workers, 250 grammes for workers (providing about 400 calories) and 500 for front-line troops. The grain in this bread was mixed with cellulose and sawdust. Fats, vegetables, meat and sugar virtually disappeared. It seemed impossible to sustain life under those conditions, especially for a person performing heavy labour in freezing temperatures. Over a million people died during this first winter of the siege, ninety per cent of these from hunger and disease.*

In order to feed the population the authorities battled to open a road across frozen Lake Ladoga to unoccupied Russia. Horse-drawn sledges made the first round trip on 20 November 1941, at a point when the city had only

---

* Figures from Nikita Lomagin, *Neizvestnaya Blokada* (The Unknown Siege), St Petersburg, 2002

two days' food supply left. Then lorries were driven across – the first convoy lost 157 vehicles. By late December 1941 trucks were bringing regular supplies across the ice, driving mostly at night, in temperatures that fell below minus forty degrees, under constant bombardment and air attack.

The authorities initially dragged their feet over evacuations. Eventually – after many thousands more had died – around half a million people, including many children, were evacuated along Military Highway 101, popularly known as the 'Road of Life'. There were many deaths along the way from shelling, aerial bombardment and drowning.

Even the heroic efforts of the drivers, loaders and guides could not bring in enough food to feed the whole city. The population also suffered from incompetent and corrupt elements in authority who stockpiled food for their own use. People continued to die in their thousands each day. It became dangerous to go out alone in the streets owing to the prevalence of cannibals. By late January 1942 the authorities announced an increase in the bread ration, but delayed issuing ration cards. At this, morale finally threatened to give way. People began to panic and the authorities came close to losing control. As a result they released more food into the city by the middle of February.

The ice road thawed at the end of April 1942, after which trucks were replaced by barges. Electric cables and an underwater oil pipeline, the 'Artery of Life', were laid across Ladoga. The Road of Life resumed operations again during the winter of 1942–43.

In January 1943 a Soviet offensive broke through the blockade and re-established a rail link to Moscow. Starvation eased in that year, helped by the planting of vegetable patches in the parks and gardens of the city. However the Germans increased their shelling and air raids, and these killed thousands more civilians.

The siege was lifted on 27 January 1944. Citizens were finally able to walk the streets without fear of air attack. A memorial plaque remains on Nevsky Prospect: *Citizens! In the event of artillery fire this side of the street is the most dangerous!*

About 300,000 troops died defending the city. Their bodies are still being recovered from the earth around St Petersburg.

Estimates vary on the number of civilian dead, from the official Soviet figure of almost 700,000 to a million and a half. Many people concealed the death of family members in order to use their ration cards. There were also unregistered people without cards, including thousands of refugees from the provinces.

Instances of cannibalism are equally hard to document. For example, the NKVD recorded seventy-seven instances of cannibalism before 12 January 1942, and 311 during the following three weeks.* The Leningrad NKVD formed a special division to combat murder for flesh and several hundred people were shot on this charge. Much more common were instances of cannibalisation of corpses. Those caught by the NKVD were also brought to trial and condemned to death. Alexander Solzhenitsyn wrote in *The Gulag Archipelago* that political prisoners were incarcerated with cannibals in the Big House on Liteiny Prospect.

The NKVD remained ultra-vigilant throughout the siege. Any complaint about 'difficulties with food supply' (the term used in their internal documents)

---

*   Nikita Lomagin, *Neizvestnaya Blokada*, St Petersburg, 2002 was regarded as anti-Soviet defeatism.[*] The war censor intercepted letters; informers in housing blocks, bread queues and at the workplace kept the NKVD appraised of the general mood.

Leningrad's population did not return to pre-war levels until the 1960s. In 1945 Leningrad was awarded the Order of Lenin and in 1965 it became a Hero City of the Soviet Union. The Road of Life forms part of the St Petersburg World Heritage site.

Before retreating the Germans looted and destroyed the most valuable palaces of the Tsars, such as the Catherine Palace at Pushkin, Peterhof, Gatchina and Strelna. Incalculable amounts of valuable art were looted and taken to Germany. Nazi leaders were put on trial for this 'cultural destruction' at Nuremburg. Incredible feats of restoration of the palaces took place after the war.

THE FINNISH WAR

Following the signing of the German-Soviet non-aggression pact in August 1939, Stalin sent the Red Army into Finland in November of that year. The Finns held off the Russians for five months, exposing Soviet military weakness to the Germans. In spring 1940 Finland signed a treaty which allowed it to remain independent while ceding a large part of Karelia to the USSR, including Valaam and the western Ladoga littoral.

THE PURGES

The murder of Sergei Kirov on 1 December 1934 triggered the great terror of the 1930s. Kirov was leader of the Leningrad party apparatus, a popular and influential

---

[*]   See above

member of the ruling elite. Stalin had begun to doubt the loyalty of members of the Leningrad apparatus. He needed a pretext for launching a broad purge. Kirov was murdered by a young assassin named Leonid Nikolaev. Recent evidence has indicated that Stalin and the NKVD planned the crime.

Stalin used the murder as an excuse for conducting a witch-hunt for alleged conspirators. Over the next four-and-a-half years, millions of innocent people were arrested – many of them for complicity in the vast plot that supposedly lay behind the killing of Kirov. One estimate says that a quarter of the population of Leningrad were arrested during those years. The arrests slowed but did not cease during the siege. In 1948 Stalin directed one of his most vicious post-war purges against the city – known as the Leningrad Affair.

THE ZHDANOVSHCHINA AND THE LENINGRAD AFFAIR

After the assassination of Sergei Kirov in 1934 Andrei Zhdanov became leader of the Leningrad Communist Party. He was in charge of the defence of Leningrad. After the war he was recalled to Moscow to become, by 1946, the leading figure in the party hierarchy after Stalin himself. His former deputy, Kuznetsov, was also brought to Moscow as a secretary of the Party Central Committee. Another Leningrader, Voznesensky, was now in charge of planning the Soviet economy and deputy chairman of the Council of Ministers.

In 1946 under Stalin's direction, Zhdanov denounced two of Leningrad's leading writers, Anna Akhmatova and Mikhail Zoshchenko, as part of a campaign against 'bourgeois formalism' in Soviet culture. He also attacked Prokofiev and Shostakovich. The director of the newly-opened Museum of the Defence of Leningrad was arrested and sent to Siberia.

This period was known as the *Zhdanovshchina*. It attacked 'formalist,' 'bourgeois' and foreign influences in art, culture and science.

By 1948 Zhdanov himself was falling from favour. In August he suffered a fatal heart attack – possibly as a result of his hard drinking, or possibly from poisoning. This tipped the balance in the Kremlin power struggle. In 1949, deprived of Zhdanov's protection, Kuznetsov, Voznesensky, and most of the siege leadership were arrested on such charges as planning to blow up the city, scuttle the Baltic fleet, and establish a new regime with British assistance.

After long interrogations and secret trials, they were shot in October 1950. The Leningrad party organisation was purged, and some 2,000 people imprisoned or exiled. The siege museum was closed, to be reopened forty years later. Important aspects of Leningrad's tragic and heroic wartime history were suppressed until after the fall of the Soviet Union, notably the role of the city's authorities during the siege.

THE GULAG

A system of forced-labour prison camps in the USSR, (from the Russian acronym GULag for the Main Directorate of Corrective Labour Camps, a department of the Soviet secret police). It consisted of 476 camp complexes. During the Stalin period (1928–1953) these held millions of inmates. Prisoners were both common criminals and 'politicals'. They worked on huge projects including the White Sea-Baltic Canal, the Moscow-Volga Canal, the Baikal-Amur main railway line, hydroelectric stations and hundreds of roads and industrial complexes in remote regions of Siberia and northern Russia. Prisoners mined coal, copper and gold and worked in the lumbering industries of the Siberian forests. Millions lost their lives through accident, hunger or disease.

After receiving a Certificate of Release, former prisoners such as Tamara Petkevich were still kept under surveillance, being obliged to register monthly with local authorities. They were usually banned from living in the largest cities in the USSR.

After the death of Stalin in 1953, and especially after the denunciation of the 'cult of personality' at the 20th Party Congress in 1956, the mass release of political exiles and prisoners began, followed by the process of their rehabilitation, which sometimes took decades. Many former prisoners did not live to see their rehabilitation. Although the Gulag was officially dissolved, the Soviet regime continued to imprison people for 'political' crimes.

APPENDIX 1

The Führer's decision on Leningrad.
Transmitted by Naval Warfare Command to Army Group North on 29 September 1941 (quoted in Max Domarus *Hitler Reden und Proklamationen* 1932–1945):

Subject: Future of the City of Petersburg.

The Führer is determined to remove the city of Petersburg from the face of the earth. After the defeat of Soviet Russia there can be no interest in the continued existence of this large urban area. Finland has likewise manifested no interest in the maintenance of the city immediately at its new border.

It is intended to encircle the city and level it to the ground by means of artillery bombardment.

Requests for surrender resulting from the city's encirclement will be denied, since the problem of relocating and feeding the population cannot and should not be solved by us.

APPENDIX 2

German Operational Situation Report 18 February 1942:
By December a large part of the population showed
hunger swellings. Increasing numbers of people were
collapsing on the streets and dying. During the course
of January the population were dying en masse. In the
evening hours corpses were pulled on hand sledges from
houses to cemeteries, where they were simply thrown
onto the snow due to the impossibility of digging. Lately
relatives are saving themselves the effort of going to the
cemetery by unloading corpses at the kerbside. In one
afternoon at the end of January a defector undertook
to count passing sledges loaded with corpses on a main
street of Leningrad. A hundred were counted within an
hour. In many cases the corpses were piled up in yards
and unfenced squares. A pile of corpses in the yard of
a bombed apartment block was two metres high and
twenty metres long. In many cases however, the bodies
are not even taken out of apartments but only placed in
unheated rooms. In air raid shelters one often finds dead
bodies that have not been removed. Also, for example,
in the Alexandrovskaya hospital there are about 1,200

corpses placed in unheated rooms, corridors and the yard. At the end of January it was rumoured that 15,000 were dying each day and that 200,000 had died in the preceding three months. This number is not too high in relation to the total population. It must be taken into account, however, that the number of dead will increase greatly with every week if the present conditions of hunger and cold continue. The food rations stored and distributed to individuals will have no effect.

In particular, children are said to be becoming victims of the hunger, namely infants for whom there is no food.

PEOPLE

ANNA AKHMATOVA (1889–1966)

Poet whose work is inextricably bound up with St Petersburg. She wrote: *The outbreak of the Great Patriotic War in 1941 caught me in Leningrad. At the end of September, when the city was already besieged, I flew to Moscow. Up until May 1944 I lived in Tashkent, hungry for news from Leningrad and the front. Like other poets, I made frequent visits to military hospitals and read verse to wounded soldiers… I never stopped writing poetry. For me it is my link with the times I live in…*

Akhmatova was effectively silenced by Stalin during the 1930s and again in the 1950s. She was nominated for the Nobel Prize for Literature in 1962 and awarded an honorary degree from Oxford in 1965. In 2006 a memorial statue of the poet was erected inside Kresty (Crosses) prison in St Petersburg.

ANNA NIKOLAEVNA ALEXEEVA (1898–1945)

Poet and teacher. A book of her letters and poems *Eto Leningrad! Smotri i Slushai! (This is Leningrad! Look and*

Listen!) was edited and published by her niece Natalia Tarasova in Petersburg in 1999. Alexeeva lived through the blockade, losing her husband and son and dying of heart failure on 3 July 1945.

OLGA BERGHOLTZ (1910–75)

Poet. In 1938 she was arrested on false charges. Pregnant at the time, her child was stillborn in prison. Her husband died in besieged Leningrad in November 1941. During the siege Bergholtz regularly read poems, stories and news over the radio.

MIKHAIL DUDIN (1916–93)

Poet. Served in the army from 1939. Took part in the defence of Leningrad and the Hanko peninsula.

KARL ILYCH ELIASBERG (1907–78)

In 1932 began conducting for the Radiokomitet's Grand Symphony orchestra. Remained in Leningrad from 1941–45. Conducted the Leningrad premiere of Shostakovich's Seventh (Leningrad) symphony on 9 August 1942.

ALEXANDER FADEYEV (1901–56)

Writer, one of the co-founders of the Union of Soviet Writers from 1946 to 1954, and active promoter of the *Zhdanovschina*.

LIDIYA GINZBERG (1902–90)

Literary critic who survived the purges, the siege and

the anti-Semitic years of the 1950s. In 1984 she published *Blockade Diary* in the Leningrad journal *Neva*.

OSIP MANDELSTAM (1891–1938)

Poet, leading member of Acmeist school. Arrested during purges and died in transit camp. Rehabilitated 1987. A minor planet is named after him.

ZHANNA METALLIDE (B. 1934)

Composer. Works include *Visch-atir The Warrior Lord* 1998. Her biography *Monolog* is written by N. Selvertsova (St Petersburg, 1999)

ALEXANDER MEZHIROV (B. 1923)

Poet, fought on Leningrad front.

IGOR MOISEYEV (1906–2007)

Widely regarded as the greatest twentieth-century choreographer of folk dance.

BORIS PASTERNAK (1890–1960)

Poet and author of *Dr Zhivago*. Under official pressure, he turned down the Nobel Prize for Literature in 1958.

TAMARA PETKEVICH (B.1920)

Actress and theatre critic. Sentenced in 1943, freed in 1950, rehabilitated in 1957. Her autobiography *Zhizn –Sapozhok Neparny* was published in St Petersburg in 1993.

ALEXANDER PUSHKIN (1799–1837)

Poet, author and national hero, regarded as the founder of modern Russian literature.

VADIM SHEFNER (1915–2002)

Poet. Fought on the frontline defending Leningrad before being transferred to an army newspaper. In 1943 his book of poems *The Defence* was published in Leningrad.

OLEG SHESTINSKII (1929 –2009)

Poet and writer born in Leningrad. Survived the siege. The quote in the foreword is taken from his short story 'Love' published in the journal *Neva,* issue 1, 1999

DMITRI DMITRICH SHOSTAKOVICH (1906–75)

Composer. His music was officially denounced in 1936 and 1948 and suffered periodic banning. Yet he remained the most popular Soviet composer of his generation and received a number of state awards.

At the outbreak of war in 1941 Shostakovich initially remained in Leningrad where he wrote the first three movements of the Seventh Symphony. In October 1941 he was evacuated to Kuibyshev (now Samara) where he completed the work. The Seventh Symphony was premiered in Leningrad on 9 August 1942. It was adopted as a symbol of Russian resistance to Nazism both in the USSR and in the west.

VLADIMIR SOFRONITSKY (1901–61)

Russian pianist best known for his interpretations of Scriabin.

GALINA VISHNEVSKAYA (B.1926)

The Soviet Union's leading opera singer, she defected with her husband Mstislav Rostropovich in 1974.

MAXIMILIAN VOLOSHIN (1877–1932)

Poet and prominent member of symbolist movement. His work is noted for its prophetic quality.

ANDREI ZHDANOV (1896–1948)

In charge of defence of Leningrad. In 1946 formulated his doctrine for the arts: 'Zhdanovschina', which eliminated foreign influences. Imposing strict government control on art and literature, he censored Akhmatova and the satirist Zoshchenko.

SOURCES

A. A. Alexeeva *Eto Leningrad! Smotri i Slushai!* (St
    Petersburg 1999)
M. M. Bobrov *Khraniteli Angela* (St Petersburg 1998)
A. N. Boldyrev: *Osadnaya Zapis'* ed. V.S. Garbuzova and
    I. M. Steblin-Kamensky (St Petersburg 1998)
Granin and Adamovich *Blokadnaya Kniga* (Moscow 1983)
Nikita Lomagin *Neizvestnaya Blokada* (St Petersburg
    2002)
T. V. Petkevich: *Zhizn – Sapozhok Neparny* (St Petersburg
    1993)
Varshavskii and Rest *Podvig Ermitazha* (Leningrad
    1985)
Galina Vishnevskaya *Galina – A Russian Story* (London
    1984)

POETRY
Piterburgskii Mirazh (St Petersburg 1991)
Let the Living Remember – Soviet War Poetry (Moscow
    1976)
Anna Akhmatova *Putyom vseya Zemli* (Moscow 1996)

FURTHER READING (ENGLISH)

Lidiya Ginzberg *Blockade Diary* (London 1995)

David Glantz *The Siege of Leningrad 1941–44* (London 2001)

Michael Jones *Leningrad: State of Siege* (London 2008)

Harrison Salisbury *900 Days* (London 1969)

Alexander Werth *Leningrad* (London 1944)